Much of Percy Seymour's work has been motivated by two convictions. The first is that the large-scale structure and dynamics of the universe are intimately bound up with life on earth and the structure of atoms. The second, an inevitable consequence of the first, is that astronomy is relevant to our day-to-day lives.

These beliefs have led him into many different branches of astronomy, and to consider the links between astronomy and the other sciences. After studying physics at Manchester University, he spent three years working out the structure of the magnetic field of the Milky Way. He then taught physics and astronomy in schools for a few years. As Senior Planetarium Lecturer at the Greenwich Observatory he introduced a series of lectures linking astronomy with the sciences and other subjects in the school curriculum – from geography and history to art and literature. His interdisciplinary approach to astronomy led him to explore the roots of astrology and the impact of navigation on the history of astronomy. He is currently Principal Lecturer in Astronomy at the University of Plymouth, where he continues to link astronomy with other disciplines, both in his teaching and his research. His other books include *Adventures with Astronomy*, *Halley's Comet*, *Cosmic Magnetism* and *Astrology: The Evidence of Science* (Arkana 1990). Some of them have been translated into several languages. He is married and has one son.

Percy Seymour

THE PARANORMAL
Beyond Sensory Science

ARKANA
PENGUIN BOOKS

ARKANA

Published by the Penguin Group
Penguin Books Ltd, 27 Wrights Lane, London W8 5TZ, England
Penguin Books USA Inc., 375 Hudson Street, New York, New York 10014, USA
Penguin Books Australia Ltd, Ringwood, Victoria, Australia
Penguin Books Canada Ltd, 10 Alcorn Avenue, Toronto, Ontario, Canada M4V 3B2
Penguin Books (NZ) Ltd, 182–190 Wairau Road, Auckland 10, New Zealand

Penguin Books Ltd, Registered Offices: Harmondsworth, Middlesex, England

First published 1992
10 9 8 7 6 5 4 3 2

Printed in England by Clays Ltd, St Ives plc
Filmset in 10/12 pt Monophoto Ehrhardt

Contents

To Dianna and Bruce

Introduction

> Why, all the Saints and Sages who discuss'd
> Of the Two Worlds so learnedly, are thrust
>   Like foolish Prophets forth; their Words to Scorn
> Are scatter'd, and their Mouths are stopt with Dust.
>
> Edward Fitzgerald, *The Rubáiyát of Omar Khayyám*

Science is news. Newspapers, magazines, radio and television all carry items, almost daily, about some new scientific discovery or theory. It is also the age of the media pundit – in the field of science, usually science correspondents, consultants and writers. Like most pundits they state their personal preferences, or dislikes, for one theory or another with authority and certainty. Some defend current scientific views with evangelical zeal, and wholeheartedly support present-day science with the unquestioning dedication that one normally associates with religious fanatics. For them scientific fundamentalism is the religion of the twentieth century. News is about what is happening here and now. The immediacy of the very latest news allows little respect for the history of science. Science journalists have done a great service to science by informing the public about the facts of present-day science, and the possible social implications of current scientific research, but many have done science a disservice by failing to clarify the doubts and uncertainties surrounding the latest discoveries and may have misled the public into accepting modern science as some new form of received 'truth'. Some of them do so because they themselves cannot cope with the doubts and uncertainties that exist in most areas of science. However, many do so because they received their science education at some institute of higher education, a university or polytechnic, which did little to expose them to the nature, history and philosophy of science. In this introduction I am going to argue that it is necessary to inform the public and especially science undergraduates about the history of science, and I am also going to explore the possibility of using the history of science to enlighten us about some of the problems facing scientific thought today. Science is very much concerned with argument and debate. In order to convey the vigorous flavour of the discussions which have gone on over the years, I shall quote the words of the chief protagonists of conflicting views on the nature and state of science.

A Role for the History of Science

Thomas Kuhn, from Harvard University, is one of the outstanding modern historians of science. In his book *The Copernican Revolution: Planetary Astronomy in the Development of Western Thought*, he says:

Each new scientific theory preserves a hard core of the knowledge provided by its predecessor, and adds to it. Science progresses by replacing old theories with new. But an age as dominated by science as our own does need a perspective from which to examine the scientific beliefs which it takes so much for granted, and history provides one important source of such perspective.

Kuhn's book *The Structure of Scientific Revolutions* is a very detailed and scholarly attempt to understand the factors that promote or retard the development of a scientific revolution. Here he puts forward an extremely convincing case for studying the history of science as a prerequisite to understanding the nature of revolutionary movements in scientific thought. At the start of the book he says:

History, if viewed as a repository for more than anecdote or chronology, could produce a decisive transformation in the image of science by which we are now possessed. That image has been drawn, even by scientists themselves, mainly from the study of finished scientific achievements as these are recorded in the classics and, more recently, in the textbooks from which each new scientific generation learns to practise its trade. Inevitably, however, the aim of such books is persuasive and pedagogic; a concept of science drawn from them is no more likely to fit the enterprise that produced them than an image of a national culture drawn from a tourist brochure or a language text.

If one can expect such a limited view of science from scientific textbooks, it is not surprising that the public's view of science, gained largely from the writings of science journalists, should be so far removed from scientific practice.

Kuhn then goes on to discuss some of the problems facing the historian of science. He points out that several years ago science historians were largely concerned with answering questions like, for example, who made this or that discovery, or who was the first to formulate a particular principle? From such research there arose the concept of science as a process of development by accumulation. He then goes on to say that, in recent years, some historians of the subject have begun to doubt the view that science develops by the accumulation of individual inventions and discoveries. He says:

Simultaneously, these same historians confront growing difficulties in distinguishing the 'scientific' component of past observations and belief from what their predecessors had readily labelled 'error' and 'superstition'. The more carefully they study, say, Aristotelian dynamics . . . the more certain they feel that those once current views of nature were, as a whole, neither less scientific nor more the product of human idiosyncrasy than those current today.

Many ancient ideas concerning nature and the cosmos are often dismissed as myth. Kuhn cautions us against such labelling:

If these out-of-date beliefs are to be called myths, then myths can be produced by the same sorts of methods and held for the same sorts of reasons that now lead to scientific knowledge. If, on the other hand, they are to be called science, then science has included bodies of belief quite incompatible with the ones we hold today. Given these alternatives, the historian must choose the latter. Out-of-date theories are not in principle unscientific because they have been discarded.

He also discusses the importance of experiment and observation to scientific belief:

Observation and experience can and must drastically restrict the range of admissible scientific belief, else there would be no science. But they cannot alone determine a particular body of such belief. An apparently arbitrary element, compounded of personal and historical accident, is always a formative ingredient of the beliefs espoused by a given scientific community at a given time.

These are some of the general ideas that are worth keeping in mind as we examine different views on the current state of science, and then compare these with the views about the state of the physical sciences that existed one hundred years ago.

Is the End of Science in Sight?

Stephen Hawking is Lucasian Professor of Mathematics in the University of Cambridge, the chair once held by Sir Isaac Newton. On 29 April 1980 he delivered his inaugural lecture, and in 1981 he wrote an article for *Physics Bulletin*, based on this lecture, and entitled 'Is the End in Sight for Theoretical Physics?'. At the start of his article he says:

In this article I want to discuss the possibility that the goal of theoretical physics might be achieved in the not-too-distant future, say by the end of the century. By this I mean that we might have a complete, consistent and unified theory of the physical interactions which would describe all possible observations.

In 1987 BBC Radio 3 ran a documentary on a new development in theoretical physics, under the title 'Superstrings: A Theory for Everything?'. During this programme the Nobel prizewinner Professor Richard Feynman was interviewed, and he was asked to comment on Hawking's statement. He had this to say:

I've had a lifetime of that, and I've had a lifetime of people who believe that the answer is just around the corner. But again and again it's been a failure ... And today, there are a large number of things that are not understood. That isn't fully appreciated, and people think they're very close to the answer, but I don't think so.

Feynman quoted two examples from the past, when physicists had thought that the end was in sight. Hawking, naturally, was also aware of these examples, and went on to say:

Although we have thought that we were on the brink of the final synthesis at least twice already ... we have made a lot of progress in recent years and there are some grounds for cautious optimism that we may see a complete theory within the lifetime of some of those present here. (Hawking, 1981)

Professor Philip Anderson, who shared the 1977 Nobel prize for physics with Professors van Vleck and Mott (for their important contributions to solid-state physics, work which forms the basis of tape recorders, lasers, transistors and modern computers), also disagreed with the views of Professor Stephen Hawking. In a letter to *Physics Bulletin*, just after they printed a shortened version of Hawking's inaugural lecture, he had this to say:

From time to time, eminent scientists take it upon themselves to proclaim the impending demise of one field or another. Such a proclamation is the inaugural lecture of the Lucasian professor . . . As my friend J. C. Phillips once said of another such statement, they are an admission by the author that 'all the problems – recognized as problems are (or soon will be) solved'. The problems which are recognized from the cloistered halls of the more mathematical departments at Cambridge are a particularly limited set . . . The rest of us take a broader view, and see a larger task, having more experience of the complexity of the real physical world . . . If Professor Hawking were not just assuming a professorship in which he can influence some of the brightest minds in England, his remarks would be a harmless bit of intellectual arrogance, sadly typical of his field. As it is, for the sake of the young, I feel it necessary to reassure them that one need not redefine theoretical physics into a null set.

Although I would agree with much of what Professor Anderson has to say regarding Hawking's lecture, I do not think it was necessary to worry about the students at Cambridge. The whole ethos of most academic environments encourages dissent, and students would not, at any university, be exposed to the views of just one professor. This point was well made by Dr Jacob Bronowski in *The Ascent of Man*, where he said:

Ancient university towns are wonderfully alike. Göttingen is like Cambridge in England or Yale in America: very provincial, not on the way to anywhere – no one comes to these backwaters except for the company of professors . . .

The symbol of the university [Göttingen] is the iron statue outside the Ratskeller of a barefoot goose girl that every student kisses at graduation. The university is a Mecca to which students come with something less than perfect faith. It is important that students bring a certain ragamuffin, barefoot irreverence to their studies; they are not here to worship what is known but to question it.

Hawking's views stand in very sharp contrast to a statement once made by one of his predecessors, Sir Isaac Newton:

I do not know what I may appear to the world, but to myself I seem to have been only a boy playing on the seashore, and diverting myself in now and then finding a smoother pebble or a prettier shell than ordinary, whilst the great ocean of truth lay all undiscovered before me.

The State of Physics at the End of the Last Century

It is illuminating to compare the present state of physics with the state of the subject in 1900. The situation at this time was extremely well stated by Gary Zukav in *The Dancing Wu Li Masters*:

In a speech to the Royal Institution in 1900, Lord Kelvin reflected that there were only two 'clouds' on the horizon of physics, the problem of black-body radiation and the Michelson–Morley experiment. There was no doubt, said Kelvin, that they soon would be gone. He was wrong. Kelvin's two 'clouds' signalled the end of the era that began with Galileo and Newton. The problem of black-body radiation led to Planck's discovery of the quantum of action. Within thirty years the entirety of Newtonian physics became a special limiting case of the newly developing quantum theory. The Michelson–Morley experiment foreshadowed Einstein's famous theories of relativity. By 1927, the foundations of the new physics, quantum mechanics and relativity, were in place.

It is not really necessary to know the details of these theories to appreciate the point that the structure of nineteenth-century physics, which seemed so certain to Lord Kelvin, was eventually replaced by new theories which stemmed from the 'clouds' that Kelvin saw on the horizon of physics. The two 'clouds' of Kelvin came from internal problems in physics. There was, however, another equally important cloud, with which Kelvin was directly involved, but which he did not consider to be important enough to mention in his speech of 1900. This time the challenge did not come from the physicists themselves; it came from geologists and biologists, and it concerned the age of the Earth. Its resolution was going to come from a completely new area of physics – the structure and behaviour of the nucleus of the atom.

The Age of the Earth

The arguments concerning the age of the earth are very well set out in a chapter on the subject to be found in A. Hallam's book *Great Geological Controversies*. Two separate traditions concerning the age of the Earth existed in European science before the rise of geology in the late seventeenth century. The first was known as eternalism and it derived from the teachings of the Greek philosophers. In this tradition the Earth and all nature were primary entities, self-generating, self-sustaining and existing from all time. In the Western world, based largely on Christian teachings, the doctrine of eternalism found little favour. The Judaeo-Christian heritage held that the Earth had been created by God out of nothing, and so it had a finite age. Using the highly developed scholarly tradition of historical research and criticism, Archbishop Ussher carried out his now famous calculation, from which he concluded that the Earth was created in 4004 BC on 26 October at 9 a.m. The methods which he used, were, as pointed out by Hallam, quite acceptable in his day and age, and even Isaac Newton had carried out similar calculations. The coming of geology was going to change all that.

When geologists started studying the formation of geological features, they came to the conclusion that a very long time span was necessary for geological processes to have formed the features which they studied. When Charles Darwin published *The Origin of Species* in 1859, he made it quite clear that for the evolution of higher forms of life from more basic forms by the processes of natural selection millions of years would be needed: 'He who can read Sir Charles Lyell's grand work on the *Principles of Geology* and yet does not admit how incomprehensibly vast have been the past periods of time, may at once close this volume.'

Darwin tried to get some estimate of the age of the Earth by calculating the denudation of the Weald in south-east England. By comparing the volume of material eroded from the dome with an estimate of the rate at which marine denudation would have removed it he obtained an approximate age of 300 million years.

One very influential physicist who did not like Darwin's estimate was Kelvin. He tried to calculate the age of the Sun assuming the supremacy of 'known physical laws'. From his calculations he concluded that the Sun had illuminated the Earth for not more than about 100 million years.

He went on to say:

What then are we to think of such geological estimates as 300 million years for the 'denudation of the Weald?' Whether it is more probable that the physical conditions of the sun's matter differ a thousand times more than dynamics compel us to suppose they differ from those of matter in our laboratories; or that a stormy sea, with possibly channel tides of extreme violence, should encroach on a chalk cliff a thousand times more rapidly than Mr Darwin's estimate of one inch per century.

Darwin was upset by Kelvin's attack, and in a letter to the Scottish geologist James Croll, he wrote:

Notwithstanding your excellent remarks on the work which can be effected within a million years, I am greatly troubled at the short duration of the world according to Sir W. Thomson [later Lord Kelvin], for I require for my theoretical views a very long period before the Cambrian formation.

By the end of the nineteenth century there was a great deal of opposition to Kelvin's ideas from geologists. One geologist, Professor Chamberlin, from the University of Chicago, went so far as to speculate that there might be other sources of energy that had not yet been discovered. He wrote:

Is present knowledge relative to the behaviour of matter under such extra-ordinary conditions as obtained in the interior of the sun sufficiently exhaus-tive to warrant the assertion that no unrecognized sources of heat reside there? What the internal constitution of the atoms may be is yet open to question. It is not improbable that they are complex organizations and seats of enormous energies. Certainly no careful chemist would affirm either that the atoms are really elementary or that there may not be locked up in them energies of the first order of magnitude ... Nor would they probably be prepared to affirm or deny that the extraordinary conditions which reside at the centre of the sun may set free a portion of this energy.

We thus see that a geologist was willing to speculate that the long time-scales required by observations in geology and biology were actually telling us something about the nature of the physical universe which had not as yet been discovered by the physicists themselves. We now know that Chamberlin was right, and that his words fore-shadowed the discovery of nuclear energy.

The phenomenon of radioactivity was discovered by Henri Bec-querel in 1886 and in 1903 Pierre Curie found that radium salts constantly release heat. It was the physicist Rutherford who saw that the release of heat by radioactive substances could increase consider-ably the physical estimates of the age of the Earth, and some years later it was discovered that the release of energy during nuclear processes occurring in the interior of the Sun could also give a much greater age for our Sun itself. In 1904 Rutherford gave a lecture on his work on radioactivity at the Royal Institution in London. He recalled the occasion in the following words:

I came into the room, which was half dark, and presently spotted Lord Kelvin in the audience and realized that I was in for trouble at the last part of the speech dealing with the age of the earth, where my views conflicted with his. To my relief, Kelvin fell fast asleep, but as I came to the important point, I saw the old bird sit up, open an eye and cock a baleful glance at me! Then a sudden inspiration came, and I said Lord Kelvin had limited the age of the earth, *provided no new source of heat was discovered.* That prophetic utterance refers to what we are now considering tonight, radium! Behold, the old boy beamed upon me.

Rutherford was in fact referring to something Kelvin had written in one of his articles, on the age of the Earth, in 1862. Here he said:

As for the future, we may say, with equal certainty, that inhabitants of the earth cannot continue to enjoy the light and heat essential to their life for many million years longer, unless sources now unknown to us are prepared in the great storehouse of creation.

Some Unsolved Problems in Current Scientific Thinking

Naturally there are many unsolved problems in modern science. In this section we will consider some of these problems. We will consider three different types of challenge to the scientific world view which we have at present. The first comes from problems in physics, the next comes from problems in the biological sciences and the final type comes from problems at the fringes of science, which are the areas sometimes referred to as psuedo-science and the paranormal.

1. Problems in Physics

Stephen Hawking, in his inaugural lecture, identified some of the problems which he considered to be important. Once again it is not necessary to know the details of the theory about which he is talking. The important point to understand is that there are still problems to be solved in the field in which he is working, which is concerned with producing a theory that will unify the fundamental interactions of physics. He thought that the most promising candidate for such a theory was one known technically as the $N = 8$ supergravity theory. He was well aware that a number of crucial calculations had to be carried out to see if the theory was scientifically acceptable:

If the theory survives these tests, it will probably be some years more before we develop computational methods that will enable us to make predictions and before we can account for the initial conditions of the universe as well as the local physical laws. These will be the outstanding problems for theoretical physicists in the next twenty years or so. But, to end on a slightly alarmist note, they may not have much more time than that.

There is another problem which some physicists see as extremely important. This involves the question of quantum reality. John Bell, who died in 1990, was one of the leading theoretical physicists whose work has highlighted the problems of quantum reality. He was able to show mathematically that if quantum theory is valid, then, under certain circumstances, it is possible for two subatomic particles to keep in touch with each other, even when separated by large distances, in a way that seems to imply a form of communication that is faster than light. Einstein's theory of special relativity says that no information can be transmitted at speeds exceeding that of light. There thus seems to be a direct contradiction between the two cornerstones of modern theoretical physics. His results are embodied in a proof which has become known as Bell's theorem, and the observational consequences of this theory have been experimentally verified. Henry Stapp, an American physicist, wrote that 'Bell's theorem is the most profound discovery of science.'

The physicist Professor David Bohm was aware of this aspect of quantum mechanics some time before Bell proved his theorem. Bohm tried to formulate a theory to explain it in his book *Wholeness and the Implicate Order*:

We have reversed the usual classical notion that the independent 'elementary' parts of the universe are the fundamental reality, and that the various systems are merely contingent forms and arrangements of these parts. Rather we say that inseparable quantum interconnectedness of the whole universe is the fundamental reality, and that relatively independently behaving parts are merely particular and contingent forms within the whole.

Nick Herbert in his book *Quantum Reality* says:

Religions assure us that we are all brothers and sisters, children of the same deity; biologists say that we are all entwined with all forms of life-forms on this planet: our fortunes rise and fall with theirs. Now physicists have discovered that the very atoms of our bodies are woven out of a common superluminal fabric.

Some physicists are not even aware of Bell's theorem, and many who do know of its existence would rather not face the fact that it presents a crisis to received ideas of physical reality. A similar situation exists in modern biology.

2. The Physical Consequences of Problems in Modern Biology

There are some biologists who believe that the major problems in biology have all been solved, and that it is really only the details which have to be filled in over the next few years or decades. One biologist who seems to support this point of view is Richard Dawkins. In his book *The Blind Watchmaker*, he says:

This book is written in the conviction that our own existence once presented the greatest of all mysteries, but it is a mystery no longer because it is solved. Darwin and Wallace solved it, though we shall continue to add footnotes to their solution for a while yet . . . I want to persuade the reader, not only just that the Darwinian world view happens to be true, but that it is the only known theory that could, in principle, solve the mystery of existence.

This is a quite extraordinary statement for a scientist to make. It is not, in any way, a scientific statement. It is Dawkins's own statement of his total religious commitment to the Darwinian world view, based on his own faith in the theory of evolution. It is also extremely arrogant to dismiss the important work that has gone on in physics, chemistry, biochemistry and molecular biology over the last century as mere footnotes to Darwin and Wallace. All this progress has made it possible to see, in much more detail, the chemical and physical processes that enable us to understand, in causal terms, how Darwinian evolution operates at the level of the genes, and through the genetic code. This point is well made by Arthur Peacocke in his book *God and the New Biology*. Here he says, when discussing whether evolution is fact or theory:

It is true that when Darwin propounded his theory the evidence for evolution was purely circumstantial rather than direct. Until the advent of modern biochemistry and molecular biology, the observations with which the postulate of evolution had to be consistent were drawn mainly from comparative anatomy and the morphology of living and extinct organisms . . . considered in relation to their locality and inferred climate and other environmental condition.

Peacocke also quoted from François Jacob:

Over and above the diversity of forms and the variety of performances, all organisms use the same materials for carrying out similar reactions, as if the living world as a whole always used the same ingredients and the same recipes, originality being introduced only in the cooking and seasoning.

Peacocke also points out that there are other controversies and unsolved problems in biology, one such being morphogenesis – the development, through growth and differentiation, of form and structure in an organism.

Morphogenesis and Morphic Resonance

Introducing the area of morphogenesis, Peacocke says:

However, there are other areas where . . . it is extremely difficult to formulate theories at all, the biological phenomena in question being baffling in their complexity and still capable of exciting the wonder which only the inexplicable, or at least the unexplained, can induce. The whole area of morphogenesis is an example, whether in its epigenetic (appearance of new structures), or its regulatory (embryonic) or regenerative (restoral of damaged structures) aspects – and the genesis of the organization of nervous systems, especially brains, is the most baffling area of all.

He points out that there are different approaches to these problems, varying from 'the determinedly reductionist' view of Francis Crick – 'the ultimate aim of the modern movement in biology is in fact to explain all biology in terms of physics and chemistry' – to the 'avowedly holistic', such as Rupert Sheldrake's hypothesis of 'formative causation'. According to Sheldrake, specific morphogenetic fields are responsible for the characteristic form and organization of systems at all levels – from physico-chemical to biological – and these morphogenetic fields are derived, through morphic resonance, from those of previous similar systems; that is, past systems influence the form of present systems acting across space and time. Peacocke identifies some problems with the theory. One of the problems which he isolates concerns the propagation of Sheldrake's fields:

... nor is he able to offer any conceptual framework of the mode whereby these 'morphogenetic fields' propagate and whether or not they do so at a speed which obeys the Einsteinian canon of not exceeding that of light. If they do not obey it, then various curious time-reversal effects should be (but are not) observed in biology: if they do not do so, why are these fields not detectable in the range of the electromagnetic spectrum?

At the end of this paragraph, Peacocke adds a very important comment:

Be that as it may, the fact that a biologist has had to resort to such a hypothesis at least emphasizes the radical and fundamental problems still facing biologists.

Sheldrake's hypothesis has to be developed further, but there is at least one physicist who is not outraged by the idea. He is Professor David Bohm, who we have already mentioned in connection with his own theory concerning the implicate order. He says this about Sheldrake's work:

The implicate order can be thought of as a ground beyond time, a totality, out of which each moment is projected into the explicate order. For every moment that is projected out into the explicate order there would be another movement in which that moment would be injected ... back into the implicate order. If you have a large number of repetitions of this process, you'll start to build up a fairly constant component to this series of projection and injection. That is, a fixed disposition would become established. The point is that, via this process, past forms would tend to be repeated or replicated in the present, and that is very similar to what Sheldrake calls a morphogenetic field and morphic resonance. Moreover, such a field would not be located anywhere. When it projects back into the totality (the implicate order), since no space and time are relevant there, all things of a similar nature might get connected together or resonate in totality. When the explicate order enfolds into the implicate order, which does not have any space, all places and all times are, we might say, merged, so that what happens in one place will interpenetrate what happens in another place.

3. Problems at the Borders: Astrology and the Paranormal

There are often problems at borders: borders between countries, cultures, communities, religions and people. There are naturally problems at the borders between science and other belief systems in general, but more so between science and what many scientists call pseudo-science, which they believe includes astrology and the paranormal. The general scientific attitude to astrology is fairly well stated by Judith Field, a historian of science:

Historians have tended to class astrology with the occult sciences . . . Indeed in our own day astrology is occult, in the sense that astrologers wilfully ignore the results obtained in other fields (postulating instead forces of types unknown and otherwise unexampled) and use techniques associated with mainstream science – such as statistical analysis – in a manner which clearly shows their incomprehension or rejection of the actual methods of science.

Field's claim that the use of statistical analysis by astrologers shows an incomprehension or rejection of the actual methods of science, is a purely personal judgement, which is totally unsubstantiated by the facts, and merely serves to demonstrate her profound ignorance of the work that has been done in this area and her reluctance to correct this ignorance by looking at the data in a scientific manner. Firstly, most of the detailed work in this field has been done by people who are not basically astrologers. Michel Gauquelin's work is perhaps the best known and most firmly established; he does not see himself as an astrologer and is very critical of most of the claims of conventional astrologers. Professor Hans Eysenck and Dr David Nias, who have both done work in this area, are psychologists at the Institute of Psychiatry of the University of London. They have said of the work carried out jointly by Michel Gauquelin and his wife Françoise: 'The work of the Gauquelins, to go no further, stands up to a careful degree of scrutiny, and compares favourably with the best that has been done in psychology, psychiatry or any of the social sciences . . .'

Professor Peter Roberts is a systems scientist and a physicist who has also done work on the statistical analysis of data relevant to astrology. He has confirmed many of the Gauquelins' results, and, with the astrologer John Addey, has extended these results to form the basis of the new harmonic approach to astrology. In his recently published book *The Message of Astrology* there is a foreword written by Brian Inglis, who recounts the following incident concerning an attempt to repeat the Gauquelins' work in America:

So scrupulously objective had the Gauquelins' work been – as Peter Roberts shows – that it was possible to repeat it in the United States in exactly the same form; and in 1977 the *Humanist* reported that the results revealed that there was no need to take the Gauquelins seriously. Only gradually did it begin to emerge that in fact the American results confirmed the Gauquelins', as six years later Kurtz and his fellow workers in CSICOP [the American Committee for Scientific Investigations of Claims of the Paranormal] had to confess ... Yet in their embarrassment at finding their preconceptions upset, they had permitted what was in effect a smear on the Gauquelins, by pretending their work had been discredited.

The work of the Gauquelins, and later work by Michel Gauquelin, establishes a link between the state of the cosmos at the birth of each individual and the personality of that individual. By demonstrating that this effect is linked to geomagnetism and that it obeys the established laws of heredity, his findings indicate that the astrological effect is unlikely to be occult. My own work has provided a basis for explaining Gauquelin's findings within the current framework of science. Thus it is unnecessary to invoke new forces, or an alternative view of reality, to explain the most important scientific findings about links between the cosmos and personality. These matters will be discussed in one of the chapters of this book.

However, my attempts to extend this type of approach to enable us to understand paranormal phenomena have failed. I now feel that to explain the evidence in this area we need to invoke something like Sheldrake's 'morphogenetic fields' (including his concept of 'morphic resonance') and Bohm's 'implicate order'. However, these concepts, as they stand, are really part of a metaphysical research programme, and do not as yet constitute scientific theories. In order to use them more effectively we have to create a conceptual model which will retain the positive virtues of current orthodox science, but will also allow us to include the attractive ideas of Bohm and Sheldrake. The main aim of the book is to develop such a theory.

Outline of a New Theory of Matter, Space and Time

In this book, I have attempted to describe total reality as existing at three different levels. First there is the well-known and immediate reality of the five senses. Sometimes this may involve supersensitivity on the part of humans or animals to one or other of these five senses. At other times it may involve the adaptation of one of the five normal senses; for example, the sensitivity of some marine species to electric fields can be seen as an adaptation of the sense of touch. The second level of reality is that which results from the response of humans and animals to magnetic fields, and this response can be used to find direction, time and location in space. It also allows one to understand some of the evidence concerning the links between human personality and the state of the cosmos at the birth of each individual. The third level allows one to understand many other phenomena which cannot be understood in terms of the first two levels of reality. This level requires a reformulation of our concepts of space and time. The main concept at the basis of this level of reality is that there are some pairs of points in space, anchored on two types of subatomic particle, which are linked by two different levels of space, only one of which is accessible to our five normal senses and our scientific instruments (which are merely means of extending and supersensitizing our five normal senses). The space known to us through our senses we will call sensory space, and the sub-space we will call extrasensory space. Different sets of laws apply to the two spaces. For example, in sensory space the speed of light is the limiting speed of all objects and information, but particles and events in extrasensory space are instantaneously linked to those particles and events with which they last interacted. This space is also the memory bank for all the past interactions of particles and events of sensory space. By developing such an approach to space and time, it becomes possible to understand a wide variety of phenomena relating to subatomic physics and to phenomena which we currently classify as paranormal.

The theory developed in this book is a completely new and independent attempt to explain the interconnectedness of subatomic phenomena, but because of its fundamental nature it also opens up the door to understanding some aspects of paranormal phenomena.

General Synopsis of the Book

The first chapter is concerned with the basic five senses, and how, without the use of scientific equipment, we can explore limited areas of our environment. The next chapter considers how we can extend the limits placed on our senses by the use of communications and scientific instruments, and the following chapter considers the sense of time as manifested in different biological organisms.

Chapters 4 and 5 contain an introduction to some necessary concepts of modern physics, including the ideas of Einstein's theories of relativity and some current ideas on the structure of matter. Chapter 6 discusses the nature of magnetism and magnetic memories in matter, and Chapter 7 discusses biological memories of responses to geophysical cycles and the consequences of these for a theory of astrology. Chapter 8 treats the subject of memories in matter, space and time.

The next four chapters apply the ideas developed in earlier chapters to an attempt to understand some phenomena which we currently class as paranormal. These chapters will include consideration of auras, homoeopathy, apparitions, telepathy, retrocognition and precognition. The last chapter also looks at the theory developed in this book and its possible connection with some ideas in Eastern religions and philosophies, and Western counterparts of these concepts.

> The danger of asserting dogmatically that an axiom based on the experience of a limited region holds universally will . . . be to some extent apparent to the reader. It may lead us to entirely overlook or, when suggested, at once reject, a possible explanation of phenomena.
>
> W. K. Clifford and K. Pearson, *Common Sense of the Exact Sciences*

Different parts of London are accessible by means of different types of transport. Pedestrian precincts are only accessible by walking, the lines between Underground Stations are only accessible by tube train and the centre line of the Thames is only accessible by boat. We live, move and have our being in space, but not all of this space is accessible to all of our five senses. The extent of space accessible to each of our senses is rather different, and so we can define a space for each of our senses by establishing their limits, in much the same way as we can define a space for each form of transport in London by giving the limits of, say, the road or rail network which serves that particular form of transport. Maps of the London Underground, for example, give in different colours the areas available to the different tube lines which serve the metropolis. In this chapter we will discuss the different areas that are available to our five senses, and we will compare this with the sensory spaces of other animals.

The Space of Touch

The space of touch is really defined by the space filled by our own bodies. This is because in order to feel something, we have to touch it with some part of ourselves. The tips of our fingers, the palms of our hands and the soles of our feet are the most sensitive areas of skin in this respect. The sense of touch can tell us about the temperature of the air or objects, it can tell us about the texture of materials and it can tell us something about the consistency of substances. To a blind person the sense of touch is extremely important, since it can be used to convey a great deal of information about the external world, and, with training, the sense of touch can be developed to the extent that the blind can read texts written in braille. Since we actually have to touch things before we can reach conclusions about them, the space of touch available to a stationary person is very limited. We can extend this space by waving our arms about, and by walking. We can considerably extend the space available to touch, by using different forms of transport on land, sea or through the air.

Extending the Space of Touch

There are other ways in which the sense of touch can be extended. The wind on our faces can tell us something about the temperature in the direction from which the wind is blowing, and if this is combined with weather maps it can also be used to deduce something about the weather conditions somewhere else on the Earth. Heat can be transmitted across empty space by means of waves called infra-red radiation. The infra-red radiation given off by an infra-red lamp, an electric radiator or a fire heats the skin on that side of the body facing the source, and the resulting sensation of warmth it produces can be used to tell us the direction of the object producing the heat. This particular way of extending the sense of touch can also give us information on the direction of the Sun when our eyes are closed, so in this case it can be extended 93,000,000 miles into space. Under certain circumstances we can even 'feel' the Moon, which is about 240,000 miles from Earth. This can happen if we are sitting on a beach, near the top of the high water mark, when the tide is out. The gravitational tug of the Moon on the waters of the ocean causes the tides, and as the Earth is spinning in the tidal envelope created by the Moon, the tide will come in. When it comes in the waters just off the coastline of our particular beach will begin to lap at our feet. We are really feeling the consequences of the effects of the Moon on the oceans.

Touch and Temperature

It is through the nerve endings in the skin that we are able to judge the temperature of objects. Spots sensitive to either cold or heat are to be found between 1 and 5 mm apart all over the skin. In comparison with some other animals, our own system of judging heat is rather unsophisticated. The Australian mallee bird, an incubator bird which resembles a turkey, incubates its eggs in a mound of rotting vegetation. This bird has a very sensitive and accurate natural thermometer in its bill, which it uses to keep the mound containing the eggs at a constant temperature of 33 degrees Celsius. Ticks can use their proboscis in a similar way, and the vampire bat has a strange convoluted patch of skin, containing heat-sensitive areas, called the nose-leaf, which it can use to find prey. Some snakes, like the moccasin and the rattlesnake, have heat-sensitive organs on either side of the face, between the nostrils and the eyes, which allow them to detect changes in temperature as small as 0.003 degrees Celsius, and thus are virtually able to 'see' a vague outline of their prey in total darkness.

Other Ways of Extending Touch Space

Animal whiskers are formed from stiff hairs, and the follicle at the base of each hair is able to detect the direction and speed of any bending that occurs. Thus these whiskers extend an animal's sense of touch beyond its body. Cats use their whiskers to negotiate narrow corridors and, in conjunction with their eyes, to build up a three-dimensional view of their surroundings. The whiskers of seals respond to nearby water movements and so help them to locate fish.

Many flying insects use their antennae to judge their speed through air. For example when a locust flies, the flow of air causes its antennae to bend outwards, giving an indication of speed. If necessary, it will reduce speed by beating its wings more slowly. In addition to the antennae, the locust also has a patch of tiny hairs on its head, which bend backwards as it flies, and so are an additional source of information on speed. This type of speed indicator will work well in still air, but if the locust is heading into a wind, it has to combine this information with visual observations of its speed across the ground. Taking into account this visual estimate of its speed, the locust will alter the angle of its antennae. If its eyes tell it that its speed with respect to the ground is too slow, then it moves its antennae closer together and beats its wings faster. The reverse will occur if it is moving too fast with respect to the ground. Birds use the way the air passing over their feathers distorts their rest positions to find the speed with which they are moving with respect to still air. In windy conditions this is combined with visual estimates of their speed.

Many animals can detect vibrations on the surface of still ponds or lakes, and then use this information for a variety of purposes. Whirligigs are small black beetles often found on lakes and ponds. They move about the surface of the water in a frenzied dance to confuse their predators, and yet they do not collide with each other. They use their divided antennae, one part of which rests on the water surface, to detect the slightest vibration of the surface. They can distinguish between their own ripples and those produced by other whirligigs by some tuning process, which must be very similar to the tuning of a radio set to pick up the programmes being broadcast by different radio stations. The whirligigs are using the ripples they make as a kind of water-surface radar. As these ripples bounce off objects they can be used to locate the objects in much the same way as a ship's radar can be used to locate other ships. The ripples produced by its prey will be different from those generated by other whirligigs, so they can be used to locate and capture the prey. Water striders also use ripples to locate prey, and to communicate with each other. The number of ripples produced per minute by the male water strider is about nine times greater than that produced by the female. This type of tuning is based on the concept of resonance, which is a physical principle we will be using throughout this book, so we will spend a little time discussing the basic ideas.

'Tuning In' and Resonance

Small regular fluctuations can have large consequences if their frequency is equal to or extremely close to the natural frequency of the system to which they are applied. This is the basis of resonant tuning. A swinging pendulum has its own natural frequency; if we apply a force to the pendulum which has the same natural frequency, then the amplitude of swing of the pendulum will gradually increase over several cycles. The same applies to a child on a swing. The main physical principle involved is that when energy is fed into the pendulum, by pushing at its own natural frequency, then each small amount of energy is remembered and stored in the system. However, if energy is fed into the system at a frequency which is greatly different from its natural frequency, then it is not remembered or stored, and as a result it has no long-lasting effect.

Many physical, biological and technological systems exhibit the phenomenon of resonance. The phenomenon is to be found on scales ranging from the very smallest physical systems right up to that of the solar system itself. It has now been established that the nucleus of the carbon atom has a resonant energy level which is essential to the process of building up the heavier chemical elements in the interiors of stars – this was a vital stage in the chemical evolution of the universe, and it made possible the eventual appearance of life on earth. Atoms and molecules respond resonantly to specific types of radiation, and ignore other types of radiation. Biological organisms respond resonantly to certain sounds and vibrations and ignore all others. Resonances between the orbital periods of the asteroids (sometimes referred to as the minor planets) and the orbital period of Jupiter seem to be connected with gaps in the asteroid belt, and resonance also seems to play a part in the dynamics of the ring systems of those planets that have such systems.

Resonance is also the basis of our systems of communication which use radio waves to transmit information over large distances, often via satellites. This point was well made by Smith and Best, in their book *Electromagnetic Man*: 'A radio receiver can detect and amplify the one very specific frequency of the transmitter to which it is tuned (a coherent signal) and which can be present in its environment at an intensity far below the overall background of electromagnetic signals from the power supply cables, other and unwanted radio transmitters, and atmospheric electricity from thunderstorms.'

On a much larger scale, a radio telescope can be tuned to receive specific radio waves emitted from hydrogen atoms in the Andromeda galaxy, which is fourteen million million million miles from our Earth.

'Tuning In' under Water

Many insects that live just below the surface of the water can use special organs in their legs to detect underwater vibrations, and these can be used to locate prey and for navigational purposes. Underwater vertebrates have even more highly developed sensitivities to under-water movements and vibrations.

There is a remarkable fish, *Astyanax fasciatus*, which lives in an extremely dark cave in Mexico, and because of the very low light levels there it has lost the use of its eyes. It uses a system of detecting disturbances in the water to locate prey, avoid predators and find its way around. Along its head and body this animal has a lateral line of sensitive hairs (attached to a jelly-like rod) which bend in the direction of any water movement. The arrangement of these hairs means that each hair picks up a slightly different impression of any disturbance, and it can use this information to build up a picture of its surroundings. This lateral-line organ is particularly highly developed in this fish, but many other fish and some amphibians have similar devices.

Water currents and the animal's own movement can mask some of the information which the animal is trying to pick up. Evolutionary changes have solved this problem for some fish by burying their lateral line in canals running along the head and body, and opening into the water through pores. This refined system can be used to improve the detail of the picture of its surroundings which it builds up. By swimming fast the fish creates a disturbance which bounces off other objects, and the reflected waves can tell the fish about the distance, direction and size of these objects. In many cases the system is tuned to the body vibrations of prey and this makes it an invaluable aid to finding food. In other cases it also helps to allow shoaling fish to maintain their position in the group.

The Space of Taste

This space is probably the most restricted of all the different sensory spaces. In our own case we generally have to have the food or drink in our mouths before we can taste it. By using our hands we can extend the range of this space because we can use them to sample different foods spread out on a table. By walking or by using other forms of transport we can extend this space because it allows us to sample food from different restaurants in our own city, country or other countries. Sometimes, to a limited extent, the wind can help us to extend our space of taste. We can sometimes taste the salt in the air blowing over the sea, or we can taste the smoke coming from a barbecue, but more often than not it is difficult to distinguish the actual taste from the smell and the memories evoked by the smell. This is because the two senses are closely interlinked. We are all aware of this interlinking every time we have a cold. The blocking of the nose affects our ability to taste our food.

Although this space is restricted, we can look at the mouth in a different way which can reveal a considerably extended taste space for some people. In this view the mouth is just the receiver for information on taste, which when linked to the memory of the individual, can reveal information on the geographical origins of food and drink. This ability is most highly developed in the gourmet and the wine expert. Their mouths are rather like taste telescopes which allow them to picture countrysides, seas and vineyards in other parts of the world. A very good description of the wine-taster in action can be found in a short story by Roald Dahl called 'Taste':

He paused, his mouth full of wine, getting the first taste; then he permitted some of it to trickle down his throat and I saw his Adam's apple move as it passed by. But most of in he retained in his mouth. And now, without swallowing again, he drew it through his lips a thin breath of air which mingled with the fumes of the wine in the mouth and passed on down into his lungs. He held the breath, blew it out through his nose, and finally began to roll the wine around under the tongue, and chewed it, actually chewed it with his teeth as though it were bread.

The importance of smell to the wine taster is even more clearly shown in an earlier quotation from the same story:

Slowly he lifted the glass to his nose. The point of the nose entered the glass and moved over the surface of the wine, delicately sniffing. He swirled the wine gently around in the glass to receive the bouquet. His concentration was intense. He had closed his eyes, and now the whole top half of his body, the head and neck and chest, seemed to become a kind of huge, sensitive smelling-machine, receiving, filtering, analysing the message from the sniffing nose.

In this particular case the space of smell was confined to the wineglass, but it can be much more extensive than this.

The Space of Smell

The sense of smell of animals is based on the ability to detect the molecules of volatile or dissolved chemicals carried to its olfactory nerves by the surrounding air or by water. Our own sense of smell is not as highly developed as that of many other animals, nor does it play such a large part in our lives. This point is also well made by Roald Dahl in another short story called 'Bitch'. In this story Monsieur Biotte explains to Monsieur Cornelius why the smell of a bitch on heat has such a great effect on the sexual desire of a dog:

Odorous molecules of a special conformation enter the dog's nostrils and stimulate his olfactory nerve endings. This causes urgent signals to be sent to the olfactory bulb and thence to the higher nerve centres. It is *all* done by smell. If you sever a dog's olfactory nerve, he will lose interest in sex. This is also true of many other mammals, but it is not true of man. Smell has nothing to do with the sexual appetite of the human male. He is stimulated in this respect by sight, by tactility, and by his lively imagination. Never by smell.

Our own sense of smell is located in an area of mucus-covered yellow tissue in our noses. This membrane contains about 10 million specialized cells, each bearing tiny hairs. As we breathe, we draw air over this membrane, and different sites on the hairs respond to the molecules of particular scent chemicals. The smell which we experience depends on which combination of these sites is triggered. To save space this membrane is in the form of many folds. Our membranes have a total area of about 4 sq. cm, most cats have an area of about 14 sq. cm, but dogs have an area of 150 sq. cm.

In many fish the senses of smell and taste are very much linked together, but their taste receptors are not, like man's, only in their mouths. Some catfish can use the taste buds that cover their bodies to locate supplies of food. They can also use their noses to detect distant sources of chemicals in the water that passes through these organs. This ability is extremely highly developed in some fish. For example, the trout can detect smell chemicals of shrimp diluted a thousand million times, and the sensitivity of the eel is a thousand million times greater than that of the trout.

Birds and many winged insects also have highly developed senses of smell. Turkey vultures can detect freshly killed carcasses through kilometres of dense forest, and the tsetse fly can detect the breath of cows over similar distances. In all cases the limits of the smell space of humans and animals are considerably altered by winds. It is a great deal easier for animals to detect scents that are upwind from them than to detect scents that are downwind. All hunters allow for this when they are stalking.

Scent is not only used to locate prey and avoid predators. It can also be used to mark the territory of some animals, such as cats. In this sense domestic toms are very similar to their much larger relatives, male lions, and will readily spray objects within the home and outside to mark the limits of their territorial space.

Several animals use their urine or special secretions from other glands to lay trails of scent as they move away from home, so they can find their way back. For example, the bushbaby urinates on its hands before it sets out into the darkness of the African night so that every step of its outward journey leaves a reminder of the way back home. Slow lorises do much the same thing. Rats and mice smear secretions from glands on their bodies on the ground, and antelopes have glands on their feet for the same purpose.

Insects, like ants and bees, also use scent trails, once they have found a source of food, to guide other members of their species to the food supply. Ants deposit scent from the tip of their abdomen along the route from food to nest, whereas some tropical bees have scouts which create an aerial path by depositing scent on the tips of the vegetation.

Salmon can find their way back to the stream in which they were spawned by identifying the proportions of different chemicals within the water, and it now seems as if birds also use the sense of smell, along with other navigational aids, to find their way back home. Although humans cannot use scent in this way, we have bred the tracker dog which can do it for us. Each of us every day sheds some 50 million cells of skin which, after rising on the warm air of our bodies, fall to the ground, thus forming a trail like that of an invisible paper-chase. Each of us has our own unique smell, rather like a scented fingerprint, which is carried by the skin paper trail we leave behind as we walk, and this can be picked up by the bloodhound once it has sniffed something that we have handled.

The Space of Sound

Just as solids can vibrate, and there can be ripples on the surface of water, or even under the water, so there are ripples in the atmosphere which we call sound waves. These sound waves are very tiny changes in the pressure of the air that propagate outwards from any object that creates a disturbance in the air. The sources of these disturbances are many and varied. They can be caused by the movement of the branches of trees in the wind, by the mouths and throats of animals, or by the movements of parts of the bodies of insects. These waves are vital to the very survival of many different species, for two reasons. They provide the individuals of these species with information about their environment, including the location of predators and prey, but they also allow at least some form of communication between the individuals of a species, even though in some cases this takes a very basic form. In all cases the organs that pick up these sound waves can only receive a limited range of frequencies, although the extent and limit of this range varies from one species to another. Even within this range, in most species, an animal responds particularly to specific frequencies emitted by its mate, by other members of its own species, and by its predators and prey.

Animals hear a similar range to the sounds we ourselves hear. Some species have more extensive ranges than we have, and so can hear sounds that we cannot hear. Elephants and pigeons can hear the very low-frequency sounds known as infrasound. At the other end of the scale there is very high-frequency sound, called ultrasound, which is used by mice and bats. The size of the animal is generally, though not always, related to the frequency to which it responds – large animals hear lower frequencies than small ones.

The frog has a very narrowly tuned range of frequencies to which it responds. To quote from *Supersense* by John Downer:

The world would sound very strange to us through the ears of a frog, for we would hear the calls of other frogs, the noises made by its predators, and little else. Its ears are only sensitive to the frequencies of these sounds and its brain will only respond to certain patterns of sound, so nearly all unnecessary noises are excluded.

Downer points out that the frequencies to which different species of frog will respond vary from one region to another, and if a female is taken to a different region, it will ignore the males of this region because it is effectively deaf to their calls. The coqui frogs of Puerto Rico are so called because the male produces a noise that sounds like 'ko-kee' to us. However, only the 'ko' part is heard by other males, announcing ownership of territory, whereas the 'kee' is a mating call and only the females respond to it. Both male and female of the species, as with most other frogs, also respond to a band of lower frequencies which allows them to detect the noise of predators.

Infrasound, the extremely low-frequency sound mentioned above, can carry for considerable distances. Sources of this type of sound are the wind blowing over mountain ranges or the sands of the desert, the breaking of waves on beaches and the machinery used in towns and cities. It is very likely that some birds become familiar with these sounds and use them to find their way home. Elephants, on the other hand, seem to use infrasound to communicate with other members of their own species over large distances.

Bats navigate by a system called echo location. We all know that under certain circumstances, for example in a dome or tunnel, or in some mountainous regions, we can hear the echo of our own voices. This echo is really the result of the sound waves we produce bouncing off the solid objects which surround us. The time delay between the sound we produce and the echo we hear can be used to tell us how far away an object is. This principle is the basis of the bat's echo location system, which it can use to build up a picture of its surroundings and to locate prey. Under normal conditions the bat produces a series of pulses at between five and twenty pulses a second; as a bat moves in on its prey it increases the rate at which it produces these pulses of sound to about two hundred per minute. If the pulses are bouncing off a moving object, then the rate at which they are received back by the bat will be different from the rate at which they are emitted. If the object is moving towards the bat, the number of pulses received per second will be increased, whereas if the object is receding the rate of the pulses will be decreased. This general physical principle is called the Doppler effect, and the bat can use it to hunt down its prey. The radar speed traps used by the police to find out the speed of cars also work on this principle.

The Space of Sight

Just as we can have invisible sound waves moving through the air, so we can have invisible ripples of electric fields moving through space. Later on in the book we will see that any changing electric field always has associated with it a changing magnetic field. This is why we call these ripples of electric and magnetic fields moving through space electromagnetic waves. The wavelengths, the distances between successive peaks of the ripples, vary a great deal. Our eyes, and the eyes of many animals, are 'tuned' to receiving a rather narrow band – which we call light – of this type of radiation. Newton showed us that by passing light through a prism, we can split the white light into the colours of the rainbow, the visible spectrum. However, on either side of the visible spectrum there are wavelengths which our eyes cannot see. Just beyond the violet end of the spectrum, we have radiation known as ultraviolet, with a wavelength slightly shorter than that of violet. Beyond the red end we have a type of radiation called infra-red, with a wavelength slightly longer than that of red.

There are many sources of light waves. During the daytime the Sun is our major source of such waves, if we are outdoors. We are able to see objects by means of the sunlight reflected off them. At night we can sometimes use the much weaker light from the Moon, which in itself is reflected sunlight, or we can use the artificial light produced by electricity. The stars produce their own light, which is much fainter because they are so far away from us. The interaction of light from our surroundings with our eyes is our major source of information on our environment.

Biological Responses to Light

Most living organisms respond in some ways to light. The response of green plants to sunlight is vital for the continuing existence of life on Earth. Some of the light waves from the sun fall on the green leaves of plants – trees, bushes and blades of grass. The leaves are made up of millions of cells, each cell containing a substance called chlorophyll. When sunlight passes into a leaf, the packets of chlorophyll contained in the cells capture the sunlight, and use this energy to power their chemical factories. These factories turn carbon dioxide and water into food which is essential for the growth of plants. This is the first part of a long food chain through which animals and humans get their energy indirectly from sunlight, by consuming vegetable matter. Plants also respond to light in other ways.

On the whole, multicellular plants cannot move about, but they exhibit bending and torsion movements as part of their response to light. There are two types of response: in the first, photonasty, light triggers the movement; in the second, phototropism, light determines the direction of movement. The most important case is that of bending towards the light, which is called positive phototropism. This particular response occurs among photosynthesizing plants for which strong illumination is necessary for survival. The light space of such plants tends to be largely extended about 93,000,000 miles in the direction of the Sun. It is not surprising, then, that many such plants should also exhibit periodic responses resulting from the spinning of the Earth on its own axis. The axis of our Earth is orientated in the same direction with respect to the distant stars, over very long periods of time. This means that during the northern winter the north pole leans away from the Sun, but during the northern summer it leans towards the Sun. This behaviour of the axis, combined with the actual spinning, not only causes day and night, and variations in the length of the day, but also causes the amount of radiation we receive from the Sun to vary with the time of year. These last two factors give rise to the seasons. The periodic responses of plants to all these changes give rise to botanical cycles. Such cycles are classified under the general heading of photoperiodism, and they are the basis of the many biological clocks which are encountered in the plant kingdom. The light responses of plants are rather crude compared with those of the animal kingdom, and they require very high levels of light. The responses of animals are much more specific and also have a much higher level of sensitivity. This has resulted from the evolutionary development of special light-sensitive areas and eyes.

Light-sensitive Areas

The ability of plants and animals to react to light comes from certain chemicals or pigments that are photosensitive, i.e. they respond in some way to light. The light-sensitive pigment of plants, chlorophyll, is to be found in the green parts of the plants. In some one-celled animals these pigments may be scattered throughout the cell, or they may be gathered together in one part of the cell to form an eye spot. Certain multicelled animals may devote whole cells to receiving light, and, once again, these may be gathered together in one or more eye spots, or they may be scattered around the surface of the body. Such light-sensitive cells are able to distinguish between light and dark, but they are unable to give very much information on the direction and intensity of the light. Some other animals, like, for example, flatworms and starfish, use a slightly more sophisticated system in which the eye spots are placed in cup-like depressions, which can be seen as 'ears of light' so the animal can get some idea of the direction from which the light is coming. Even insects that have well-developed eyes may retain simple basic eye spots as well. For example, on either side of its head the dragonfly has some eye spots which can only distinguish between the light of the sky and the darker ground, and are used in flight as an horizon indicator to enable the dragonfly to keep a level course.

Simple Eyes

The simplest eyes are based on the physical principles of the pinhole camera, which does not have a lens. Such a camera can be easily made out of a small box, with a pinhole in the centre of one face and a light-sensitive plate on the inside of the opposite face. One marine creature that has an eye rather like the pinhole camera is the nautilus. This mollusc gets its buoyancy and protection from the multi-chambered shell in which it lives. The light-sensitive area of each of its pinhole-like eyes has about four million light receptors, and the 'pinhole' is an opening which can vary in size from 3 to 0.4 mm. When this hole is at its smallest, the image is sharp and distinct, but in the low light levels in which this organism exists, it is often necessary to have the hole wide open to gather as much light as possible. Then there are a number of overlapping images and the general picture is unclear. This problem is overcome in the eye of the octopus by the use of a lens which can be moved to bring the image into focus. Many other animals also have lenses on their eyes for the same reason.

Eyes with Lenses

Most vertebrates have eyes that resemble, in some respects, the construction of cameras. In all modern cameras a lens in front of the shutter refracts the light, and, when the shutter is open, it will bring the light rays into focus on the film, provided the distance between the lens and the film has been properly adjusted. The amount of light entering the camera can be varied to suit the lighting conditions by adjusting the aperture of the camera. In our own eyes light passes through the cornea (the lens) and then through the pupil, the hole in the iris (diaphragm), which is the part that gives the eyes their distinctive colour, before falling on the retina. The size of the pupil can be varied to suit the light conditions, and the focusing is done by changing the curvature of the lens. The retina changes the light impulses into nervous signals, which are then transmitted to the brain. Because we have highly developed brains we are able to fill in a great deal of detail.

The eyes of some more primitive vertebrates carry out a filtering function, so much of the information does not get to the brain. Each eye of the frog has a range of different nerve cells in its retina, and these respond to different types of stimuli. Some are triggered by the movements of objects of the right size and these are used to detect flies, while others can respond only to moving edges.

Colour-coding Light Waves

The retinas of our own eyes have two different types of receptors, rods and cones. The cones are of three kinds, each kind being mainly sensitive to a different colour of light. One kind is sensitive to yellow-green and red light, one to green light and one to blue. The information sent by the retina to the brain by the different cones is processed to produce a complete colour picture which contains many different hues. Some other primates, for example gorillas and baboons, have eyes similar to our own, and we believe that these animals see the world much as we do. Earlier on in this chapter, we mentioned pigments in connection with light-sensitive spots. These pigments are chemical substances which respond to light, and are contained in the cones. In the more developed eyes of many animals, the colour coding is achieved by the use of different pigments which respond selectively to particular colours, or, to put it a different way, react 'resonantly' to particular wavelengths of light. People who are colour-blind have one of the pigments missing from their cones. Some fish and birds have five different pigments, and so see a greater range of hues than we do.

Responding to Polarized Light

Another property of light to which some animals can respond is that of polarization. Since light can, as we have already noted, be seen as a wave phenomenon, with the waves vibrating at right angles to the direction of motion, it is possible to produce waves that are vibrating preferentially in one direction. This can be done by passing the waves, which are normally vibrating in all directions, through a special polarizing filter which will block most of the waves, but will allow through those that are vibrating in the chosen direction. As the light from the Sun passes through our atmosphere, some of it is polarized at right angles to the direction in which it is moving. This gives rise to a pattern of polarized light in the sky; this moves around with the Sun and thus can be used to locate the Sun's position. For millions of years bees have used this pattern as a navigational aid.

The polarization of the sky is detected by the bees through ommatidia, which occur near the tops of their compound eyes. Although our eyes are not able to detect polarization, the Vikings used the polarization of the sky to navigate by, by using a crystal, known as sunstone, which will only transmit light when held at certain angles. This crystal enabled the Viking navigators to determine the polarization of the sky, and hence find the direction of the sun, even on cloudy days, or when the sun was below the horizon. A more sophisticated application of this principle led to the development of the Pfund sky compass, which was used by pilots in the Second World War when flying near the north pole at times when the sun was not visible.

The Sixth Sense

It is not easy to find a definition of the so-called sixth sense. However, the subject has been mentioned in recent years by two authors.

In the first chapter, entitled 'Sixth Sense', of his book *Supersense*, John Downer writes:

We experience our surroundings through the five main senses of sight, hearing, touch, taste and smell. For many centuries people assumed that other animals had a similar, if perhaps more limited, view of the world. Any strange or inexplicable behaviour, both in humans and in the natural world, was put down to some supernatural sixth sense.

The subject is also briefly mentioned by R. Robin Baker in his book *Human Navigation and the Sixth Sense*. In the preface to this book, Baker points out that in 1873 the journal *Nature* invited contributions on the mysterious and instinctive sense of direction in some animals and in man. He then adds, 'There were many notable contributors, among them Charles Darwin. The articles crystallized a belief that has persisted in many quarters until the present day: animal navigation makes use of some form of "sixth sense".'

At least some of the phenomena which at one stage were believed to indicate the existence of a sixth sense could be understood once we had a theory of sound waves and once we realized that the range of frequencies to which our ears are tuned was not necessarily the same as for other animals. Again, once James Clerk Maxwell had published a theory of electromagnetic radiation we realized that light was just a small part of a vast spectrum of electromagnetic radiation, with the extremely short gamma rays and X-rays at one end and infra-red radiation and radio waves at the other. We then discovered that some snakes and fish can detect infra-red radiation and many birds, some fish and a few insects can detect ultraviolet radiation. However, not all examples of mysterious abilities in the animal world can be explained in these terms.

Some animals have the ability to detect and generate electricity. Our own bodies work on electricity. Nerve impulses are really electrical messages carried along the nervous system, and muscle cells are activated by electricity. Medical practitioners can diagnose some diseases of the brain and heart by studying the electrical activity of these organs using special equipment. We are, however, unable to detect the electricity generated by another person without this equipment.

Water is a fairly good conductor of electricity, and some underwater animals have the ability to tune into the body electricity of their prey in particular. One such animal is the duckbilled platypus, a mammal which lives in lakes and streams in Australia. This mammal has electric sensors in its bill which are able to detect an electric field as weak as a 500 millionth of a volt per centimetre (0.05 microvolt). Some fish, like sharks, are able to detect the electricity generated by muscle movements of the prey, whereas others, like rays, generate their own electricity and gather information on their surroundings from the way this field is distorted by objects with different electrical conductivities. This electric field is generated by modified muscle cells, and in the case of the electric eel these cells can generate up to 550 volts, enough to stun or even kill their prey.

Our senses help us to navigate our way around our environment. The senses also help animals to recognize their own species, to find mates and prey, and avoid predators. The young of many species use their senses to map their environment and their relationship to their environment. These senses carry information to the developing brain, and reveal to the young that some parts of their world are actually attached to them and other parts are separate from them. Thus they learn that they look, smell, sound, taste and feel different from other members of their species, and also from other parts of their environment. This awareness of separateness is an essential part of the growth process. The same senses can be used as a method of communication between the individual members of a given species. We can also use our senses to explore the nature of the world around us by inventing instruments and devices which extend the range of our senses. Such instruments help us to overcome the limits on our sensory space which result from evolutionary adaptations to that part of the environment which was necessary for our survival. These matters will be discussed in the next chapter.

2 | Sensory Communication and Exploration

> For in and out, above, about, below,
> Tis nothing but a Magic Shadow-show,
>   Play'd in a Box whose Candle is the Sun,
> Round which we Phantom Figures come and go.
>   Edward Fitzgerald, *The Rubáiyát of Omar Khayyám*

The world revealed to us by our senses is largely a subjective one. The way each one of us reacts to sensory stimuli is different. Science is an attempt to produce, as far as is possible, an objective view of the world. In order to do so we need to compare our own various perceptions of the world with those of others, so we need methods of communication. We also need instruments that can make measurements of the external world. Some of these instruments can help us to increase the range of our senses. In this chapter we will discuss the use of communication and exploration for building up more objective world views.

Communicating via the Senses

To a limited extent all our senses can be used for communication. In a general way we can consider communication as a way of extending our sensory spaces. However, although the senses of touch, taste and smell are used by some animals for communicating with other members of their own species, for us the senses of hearing and sight offer the greatest opportunities of extending the spaces accessible to our experience.

Prehistoric Communications

Our ears and our voices determine how much sensory space is available to us for communication. In modern times this has been greatly extended by technological developments such as radio, telephone and radar. But in prehistoric times people discovered that they could communicate over longer distances by, for example, beating with sticks on hollow logs or tree trunks. From this, drums were developed, and later, using this experience, people used such things as reed pipes, rams' horns or bone whistles to communicate in a more sophisticated way. This way of transmitting messages did not use writing, and is therefore called non-alphabetic signalling. Rhythms and intonations may represent emotions or ideas, and pre-arranged notes or sequences of notes may convey simple messages.

Fires were also used throughout history for visual signalling. The Picts are said to have lit signal fires to warn of Roman invaders in Britain in the first century. Some American Indians in Ohio transmitted messages by means of smoke signals. It is said that the message of the fall of Troy in the thirteenth century BC was brought to Queen Clytemnestra by means of nine beacon fires lit upon high hills, relaying the news over a distance of about 500 miles.

Alphabetic Communication

It is possible to send optical messages over large distances by coding letters of the alphabet into various combinations. This takes the idea of beacon fires to a further level of sophistication. According to Polybius, the Greeks developed such a method in about 300 BC. The twenty-four letters of the Greek alphabet were placed in a grid of twenty-five squares, arranged in five rows and five columns. Alpha, the first letter, was in the first row of the first column; and omega, the last letter, was in the fifth row of the fourth column. All the letters could be transmitted using ten vases, placed on two low walls, the walls standing for either 'row' or 'column'. Thus, if one vase was placed on each wall it would stand for the letter alpha, but if five vases were placed on the left wall and four on the right, it would indicate the letter omega.

Much nearer to our own time, optical telegraph systems were developed which used the same general principle. Semaphore was developed for the First Republic in France in 1794, by two brothers called Chappe; and in England in 1795 the Admiralty developed the shutter telegraph. The semaphore equipment consisted of a horizontal regulator beam with an indicator arm at each end. The beam could be either horizontal or at an angle of 45 degrees to the horizontal, and the arms could each be set, independently of the beam, in vertical or horizontal positions or at angles of 45 degrees. This gave forty-nine possible combinations to represent letters or symbols. Such semaphore devices were usually located on hilltop towers, and the station fitted with a telescope – in this way messages could be relayed from one hilltop to the next. The shutter telegraph, invented by George Murray, an English bishop, consisted of six shutters which could be turned to either horizontal or vertical positions. The shutters were arranged in a two by three pattern, such that when a shutter was vertical it was visible to a distant observer, and when horizontal it was not. This system gave sixty-four possible combinations to code letters, numbers and other symbols. The Murray system spread to America, and the hilltop locations of relay stations are still marked on maps as a telegraph hill or signal hill. At one time a Murray line, used mainly by merchants, formed a communications link between New York and Philadelphia.

Electric Telegraphy and Radio

The discovery of electric current, and its magnetic effects, was the basis for telecommunications as we know it today. In the first telegraph system, an electric wire was passed over a magnetic compass and when a current was passed through the wire it caused the compass needle to move. Samuel Morse developed his well-known system from this newly discovered principle. A key was used to pass current through the wire, which caused a magnetic arm to move, and this movement caused a stylus to make marks on a moving paper tape. The mark made by the stylus on the paper tape depended on how rapidly or slowly the key was depressed, giving rise to dots and dashes on the tape – thus Morse code was devised to represent letters and symbols.

In 1876 and 1877, Alexander Graham Bell patented a device which allowed the sound waves from the human voice to cause a diaphragm to vibrate; these vibrations were made to modulate the current passing through a wire and this modulated current was, in turn, used to cause a distant diaphragm to vibrate in unison with the first. The modern telephone is a development of Bell's invention.

The Scottish physicist James Clerk Maxwell, building on the experimental work of Michael Faraday, proved mathematically that electric and magnetic energy travels in waves at the speed of light. This important theoretical result was demonstrated experimentally by Heinrich Hertz, at least over short distances, and further developed by Marconi, who turned the waves into a method of transmitting Morse code and signals without the need for electric wires. Thus radio was born, and we had a method of increasing considerably our audio communications space. By using earth satellites as radio-wave relay stations, in much the same way as hilltop relay stations were used in early optical telegraphy, we have now extended our communications space to encircle the globe.

Cosmic Exploration via the Senses

Communication requires the active participation of a transmitter and receiver. Some of the methods used for communication can also be used to expand our sensory spaces, since they can passively receive information from objects that emit radiation or sound. In this section we will discuss how this can be achieved.

1. Optical Exploration

In the last section we saw that the telescope was an integral part of some of the methods of sending light signals from one hilltop station to the next. The telescope can be considered more generally as a method of extending our visual space. The sensitivity of our eyes is limited by the intensity of the light needed to activate the optic nerve and by the size of the pupils of our eyes. In low light levels the size of our pupils increases to allow more light to enter, but this increase is limited by the dimensions of the eye. The pupil size also determines the detail we can see in distant objects. The main lens or mirror of a telescope gathers a great deal more light than our eyes are able to, and, because its diameter is greater than the maximum size of our pupils, it also allows us to see more detail in distant objects. It is then not surprising that the telescope played such a great part in the early history of astronomy; it will continue to be an important instrument for extending our sensory space far beyond the limits imposed on it by our eyes.

Galileo and the Telescope

In 1609 Galileo heard that a device, consisting of two tubes with lenses at either end, had been invented in Holland, and with this instrument it was possible to get closer views of distant objects. Within a few months of hearing this report Galileo had made his own telescope, and with this he made a number of discoveries that strengthened belief in the heliocentric Copernican system.

Galileo discovered that the surface of the Moon was full of craters and mountains, and that it resembled, in parts, the surface of the Earth. He found dark patches on the Sun – which we now call sunspots. Here was an example of imperfection in the heavens. Galileo was also able to see that Jupiter had four moons, and that these moons circled the planet, proof that there were bodies in the universe that circled round an object other than the Earth. The fact that Venus showed phases – similar to the phases of the Moon – was another important discovery, which indicated quite clearly that Venus was going round the Sun. He also showed that the Milky Way consisted of a very large number of stars, and since these stars showed no movement as the Earth moved round the Sun, they must lie well beyond the planet Saturn.

By providing a new tool for astronomers, and using it with great effect, Galileo was to give a tremendous boost to the reform of astronomy as a science.

After the initial work of Galileo, others developed the telescope a great deal further and this led to more important discoveries in astronomy. Isaac Newton invented a telescope in which a concave mirror collected the light and focused it on an eyepiece. There were also developments in lens telescopes and the mounting of telescopes. Many of these improvements were introduced by the makers, who also made navigational and surveying instruments. These improvements extended still further the limits of our visual space, and by so doing clarified the position of our solar system in the universe.

William Herschel built some of the largest early telescopes making use of mirrors, although his mirrors were made of specula metal, whereas modern mirrors are made of glass. With one of these telescopes he found the first planet to be discovered with a telescope – the planet Uranus. He then went on to make a considerable advance in the study of the structure of our Milky Way Galaxy of stars, and he also observed that many stars occurred in pairs – called binary systems – and that they orbited around their centres of mass.

The Impact of Photography and Electronic Devises

The invention of photography provided astronomers with a means of detecting objects a great deal fainter than those that could be seen by the human eye, even when assisted by large telescopes. The sensitivity of the eye is limited by the amount of light energy that can activate the optic nerve in fractions of a second, but the photographic plate or film can accumulate light energy over a period of several hours by using long exposure times. The building of telescopes with very big mirrors in America, and the use of photography, gave us a better appreciation of the scale of the 'observable universe' during the 1920s. These telescopes were also used to make the discovery that the most distant galaxies were receding from our own with speeds that were proportional to their distances from us. In other words, the further a galaxy was from us the faster it would be moving away. These observations, combined with Einstein's theory of gravitation (the general theory of relativity), led to the concept that the universe was expanding, and that the whole cosmos probably started with a 'Big Bang'.

In recent years electronic devices have been invented which are even more sensitive to light, and these devices, combined with a variety of improved telescopes, have enabled us to study the light from objects that may have been formed very near the origin of our universe. Although light travels very fast, its speed is finite, so we do not see distant objects as they are now, but as they were a long time ago. This means that telescopes are a bit like time machines, and the electronic devices that record the images of distant objects are really probing the early memories of the universe.

2. Other Methods of Cosmic Exploration

In an earlier chapter we saw that light is just part of the electromagnetic spectrum. The invention of radio meant that we could use the longer waves of this spectrum to communicate with each other over large distances. It also meant that we could build special types of aerials – called radio telescopes – which could receive the radio waves emitted by many celestial objects. This led to the birth and subsequent development of radio astronomy. Our atmosphere absorbs some of the wavelengths of the electromagnetic spectrum more than it does others. Infra-red radiation can be absorbed in this way, so if we wish to study the universe using this type of radiation we have to place our infra-red telescopes up on high mountains, or we have to place them on satellites orbiting the Earth high above our atmosphere. Ultraviolet radiation, and the very short wavelength radiations known as X-rays and gamma rays, are also largely absorbed or scattered by the atmosphere, and can only be studied by placing special devices, sensitive to these types of waves, on board satellites. In this section we will look at how the new astronomies, based on these wavelengths of radiation, have increased our understanding of the structure, evolution and possible origin of the universe, and thus how they have extended our electromagnetic sensory space.

Radio Astronomy

Radio astronomy started when Karl Jansky, working at the Bell Telephone Laboratories in America, was working on identifying the source of some of the interference on radio transmissions. He was able to show that at least some of this interference was coming from radio emissions which originated in the Milky Way. Initially optical astronomers took very little notice of his discovery, and it was left to an amateur radio astronomer, Grote Reber, to take the subject further. Just after the Second World War, however, some astronomers came to realize the importance of this and other discoveries, and radio astronomy then developed very rapidly. The main areas of astronomy to which radio exploration of the universe contributed in its early days were solar physics, the discovery of a magnetic field around Jupiter, the radio emissions coming from gas, charged particles and magnetic fields between the stars of our own Galaxy, and the radio emissions coming from other galaxies. In recent decades radio astronomers have discovered rapidly rotating neutron stars (called pulsars), very distant intense sources of radio emission (called quasars) and the radio whispers of the explosion that gave rise to the origin of the universe (the Big Bang). The great importance of these last two discoveries is that they increased considerably the dimensions of our sensory space, and put us in closer touch with the early universe.

Radar astronomy is the branch of radio astronomy in which a

radio telescope is used to reflect radio waves off other objects in the solar system, like the Moon and planets; the time delay and the changes in the nature of waves received (as compared with the waves emitted) can be used to improve our understanding of these objects. Because of the great power needed to emit radio waves that can be received back on Earth after reflection, and because of the time delays involved, this type of astronomy is restricted to solar-system studies, and hence it has not extended our sensory space in the way that radio astronomy has.

Infra-red, Ultraviolet and X-ray Emissions

The development of satellites orbiting the earth meant that we could place special instruments on board these satellites to investigate the infra-red, ultraviolet and X-ray emissions from extraterrestrial objects. Although these astronomies are contributing a great deal to our understanding of these objects, they have not done very much, up to the present time, to extend our appreciation of the dimensions of the observable physical universe. However, these branches of astronomy are still in their infancy, and they may yet make discoveries that will change our understanding of space and time.

Cosmic-ray Physics

Coming to us from all directions are very-high-energy subatomic particles. Astronomers believe that they have originated in the explosions of very massive stars (these are called supernova explosions), and in other violent events in the universe, like, for example, explosive events affecting whole galaxies. The collection and analysis of these particles have considerably increased our understanding of the basic nuclear processes that are responsible for the fuelling of most cosmic objects. The world of the atomic nucleus is a microcosmos of its own, and yet cosmic-ray physicists and astronomers can help us to understand this world by studying particles coming from distant objects.

Meteor Astronomy

The Earth is continually bombarded by solid particles, of varying sizes, but all consisting of large collections of atoms which originate in the spaces between the bodies of our solar system. Most of these particles burn up in the upper atmosphere as a result of the heat generated by friction with our atmosphere, as they collide with the atoms and molecules of the gases which constitute the air. When they do so they leave a trail of incandescent gases, which will be seen as a meteor against the darkness of the night sky. (Sometimes meteors are, erroneously, called shooting stars.) The particles which produce these trails are called meteorites, and the smaller ones are called micro-meteorites. The very large meteors will survive the heat treatment in the atmosphere, and occasionally they collide with the solid earth. Several of these meteorites have been recovered, and the chemical analysis of these bodies can tell us something about the chemical composition of the early solar system, which has been fossilized in the particles. Meteor astronomy has thus extended our knowledge of remote parts of the solar system and its evolution. Events fairly remote in space and time can now be investigated using chemical analysis in a laboratory.

Exploring the Microcosmos

In order to understand the present structure, past evolution and possible origin of the universe and its constituent parts we also have to know a great deal about the behaviour of matter on the very smallest scale. This point was well made by the great astronomer Sir Arthur Stanley Eddington in his book *The Internal Constitution of the Stars*, first published in 1926: 'The inside of a star is a hurly-burly of atoms, electrons and ether waves. We have to call to aid the most recent discoveries of atomic physics to follow the intricacies of the dance. We started to explore the inside of a star: we soon find ourselves exploring the inside of an atom.'

The reasons for this need to link the microcosmos and the macro-cosmos are easy to understand. First the laws that govern the be-haviour of matter and radiation are universal laws – they are the same throughout the universe – so this means that the physics we discover in terrestrial laboratories is the same as that which governs the evolution and structure of the universe.

It is worth clarifying at this stage the sense in which the word universal is being used. Physical laws are in some ways similar to mathematical theorems, in that provided certain conditions are satis-fied then particular consequences will follow. In this century we have discovered that Newton's law of gravitation and his laws of motion have to be replaced by Einstein's general theory of relativity when dealing with strong gravitation fields and when we are dealing with the very large distances which separate galaxies. Newton's laws of motion also have to be modified by the mathematics of special relativity when we are dealing with fast-moving objects. The rules of quantum mechanics replace Newtonian ideas when dealing with sub-atomic phenomena. This does not alter the statement that physical laws are universal, because we know which laws to use, whenever the appropriate physical conditions apply, in any region of the universe. This means that although physical laws do depend on the physical conditions prevailing in a given region, they are not dependent on the location of the region, provided certain physical criteria are met.

Secondly, the radiation we receive at the surface of the earth comes to us in a coded form and the key to this code lies in the known laws of physics. The question then arises of the means available to us for exploring the microcosmos, either using our ordinary senses or extending these in some way to cope with 'seeing' things on such an extremely small scale. Let us investigate some of the possibilities.

The Optical Microscope

The application of lenses to the study of the very small, by M. Malpighi, A. van Leeuwenhoek and R. Hooke, led to the invention and development of the microscope. With this instrument it was possible to discover a great deal about the nature of microscopic life. In the hands of van Leeuwenhoek and others it led to the discovery of the nature of bacteria, the existence of red blood corpuscles and the cellular nature of living tissue. Its further development led to the discovery of the intricacy and complexity of living organisms, and thus it played a great part in the scientific development of biology. However, it did have its limitations, and, because of the nature of light and the sizes of atoms, it could not be used to probe the internal structure of the atom. Other techniques had to be developed to accomplish this.

Probing the Atom

Ernest Rutherford, working at Manchester University in the first two decades of this century, decided to fire the subatomic projectiles called alpha particles at gold foil to see how they would be scattered by the foil. He reasoned that the way they would be scattered could be used to tell us something about the internal structure of the atom itself. Earlier on he had shown that there were three types of radiation, alpha particles, beta particles and gamma rays. He also later demonstrated that alpha particles were the nuclei of helium atoms, that beta particles were electrons and that gamma rays were very short electromagnetic waves similar to X-rays. His experiments, with H. Geiger and E. Marsden, led to a complete new branch of physics, which we now call nuclear physics. These investigations showed Rutherford that the atom consisted of a dense and massive central nucleus in which the major part of the mass of the atom was concentrated, that this nucleus had a positive electric charge and that this was orbited by a family of electrons. In other words, he thought that the atom could be modelled by a system that resembled the planets orbiting the Sun, with the nucleus as the Sun and the electrons as the planets. However, this model had one major drawback – according to the laws of physics, as they were understood at that time, the electron would radiate energy as it orbited the nucleus, and as it was losing energy it would eventually spiral into the nucleus. The fact that atoms are stable for a long time, and that they do not normally change size, shows us that electrons do not do this.

It was the physicist Niels Bohr who was to improve on the model of the atom proposed by Rutherford. By building on the work of Max Planck and on some of Albert Einstein's ideas, Bohr was able to show that the laws which govern motion on the subatomic level are different from the laws of motion of large-scale objects, like planets, which are well described by Newton's laws of motion. He further showed that by applying a revised set of laws to the motion of electrons around the central nucleus of the atom, it was possible to understand why the atoms of each element gave off, or absorbed, a definite set of colours, called spectral lines. Thus Bohr laid the foundations for using these identifying features of atoms to tell us something about the internal structure of the atom itself.

Probing the Structure of Molecules

Atoms join together to form larger structures called molecules, which are the basis of many of the complex chemicals used in the home and in industry, and they also form the chemical basis of life itself. These structures are too small to be seen with ordinary microscopes, so they have to be studied with the aid of X-rays. This form of electromagnetic radiation can be scattered off collections of molecules, and the way in which it is scattered can be used to tell us something about how the different types of atoms are arranged in molecules. At first this method was used to study the molecular structure of simple molecules like common salt, but later on it was also used to work out the structure of complicated biological molecules like the proteins and DNA, the chemical basis of genetics. This led to a great leap forward in our understanding of how the structure of molecules was related to their biological functions.

Probing Biological Structures by Means of Electrons

Electrons in motion are deflected by magnetic fields, and this means that we can use magnetic fields to focus electrons in much the same way as light can be focused by lenses made of glass. Such magnetic lenses are used around television tubes, to focus electrons from the electron gun at the back of the tube and so build up the picture on the screen. Electrons can also be transmitted through very thin sections of biological organisms, or reflected off specimens, to reveal the spacial structure of these objects. This is what is done in the electron microscope. This instrument has revealed details of structures within living organisms that could not be seen with an optical microscope, and as a consequence we have learnt a great deal more about the structure of living tissue. This type of instrument has considerably extended the limits of our sensory space, far below that set by the optical microscope.

Extending the Range of Our Experiences

Normally we experience only a limited range of temperatures, pressures and densities, and we respond only to a limited range of sound frequencies and electromagnetic wavelengths. We have already seen that we can use scientific instruments to extend the range of our sensory experience. However, if we wish to understand the behaviour of matter and material objects, and if we wish to know the limits placed on the theories which we have constructed, we need to extend the conditions under which we investigate scientific principles. For example, we were able to realize that steam, water and ice were manifestations of the same molecules of water at different temperatures only after we had investigated the nature of water in laboratories where we were able to produce a range of temperatures under controlled and measurable conditions.

Laboratories contain burners and furnaces for increasing the temperatures of substances, on the one hand, and special refrigerators for lowering temperatures, on the other. In our laboratories we can use vacuum pumps and containers to study matter under low pressures, and presses to study its behaviour at high pressures. These studies have shown us, over and over again, that many of the theories which we have formulated to deal with scientific problems at the commonplace level of experience were not always valid when we extended the range of our experiences in this way. Many scientific experiments in laboratories are concerned with such investigations.

One of the most important justifications for studying astronomy is that it allows us to use the whole universe as a laboratory, which can considerably extend the range of our senses. Although we do not have direct access to the interiors of stars, we can combine astronomical observations of starlight with the known and tested laws of physics, via mathematical analysis, to investigate the behaviour of matter under higher temperatures and pressures than we can produce in the laboratory. The spaces between the stars allow us to investigate the behaviour of matter under density conditions far lower than we can get in a good vacuum chamber on the Earth's surface. When we look at very distant objects we are also looking back in time, and so by studying these objects we are investigating the validity of physical laws and the behaviour of matter over distances and time-scales that are not available to us on the Earth. There are many examples to illustrate the fact that the study of the extraterrestrial universe has added to our understanding of the behaviour of matter and the laws of physics which govern this behaviour.

This passage from Block One of an Open University course, 'Matter in the Universe', gives a few illustrations:

But though the norm is for physics and chemistry to be applied to astronomical problems, the very different conditions in the cosmos from those on the

Earth have, on several occasions, helped to establish new physical and chemical ideas. For example, observations of the satellites of Jupiter in the seventeenth century showed that light does not travel at an infinite speed, but at a finite speed. More recently, in the early years of this century, observations of the motion of Mercury compiled over the preceding centuries, were used to help confirm Einstein's general theory of relativity . . . In 1868, the element helium was discovered spectroscopically in the Sun's atmosphere before it had been found on Earth, and in recent decades, observations of the interstellar medium have enhanced our understanding of certain types of chemical processes.

Further examples will be found in my book *Cosmic Magnetism*.

In this chapter we have seen how it is possible to extend our sensory spaces through the use of methods of communication and the methods of scientific investigation. The methods of science, and developments in technology, have not only given us a means of investigating the distribution of matter and radiation in the external universe, but have also allowed us to investigate the spatial structure and distribution of matter on the small scale, and to reveal the links between the microscopic and macroscopic worlds. Much of what has been said in this chapter is eloquently expressed in the following quotation from *Mind in Science* by Richard Gregory:

It seems that there is two-way traffic between perception and knowledge: between appearance and accepted reality. Technology extends the senses and the mind by setting up models for drawing analogies by which invisible relations, structures and laws may be discovered. At the same time it provides instruments so that the observer may be fed with quite new signals or data . . . As science becomes 'objective' so the observer disappears. And yet new observations such as Galileo's out of the blue change for ever our seeing and understanding.

Our senses reveal to us the physical cycles of our environment. Biological evolution has brought about internal cycles in organisms which match some of the periods found in our geocosmic environment. The mechanisms responsible for these internal cycles are known as biological clocks. These clocks provide us with a sense of time. In the next chapter we will discuss the sense of time in biological organisms.

3 | The Sense of Time

Come, fill the Cup, and in the Fire of Spring
The Winter Garment of Repentance fling:
 The Bird of Time has but a little way
To fly – and Lo! the Bird is on the Wing.

Edward Fitzgerald, *The Rubáiyát of Omar Khayyám*

Time and space are intertwined. At the frontiers of physics – in the theories of relativity of Albert Einstein – these two entities have been united in a fundamental way that has completely changed the way we see the physical universe. At a more day-to-day level modern methods of communication have made it necessary to consider time in other parts of the world when making a long-distance phone call, and we have had to learn to cope with jet lag when returning by air from distant parts of the globe.

Although this appreciation of the very close links between time and space is new, human consciousness of the links has been growing over the last four to five hundred years – in fact ever since it was realized that in order to find longitude, accurate methods of time-keeping had to be developed. However, even before the development of mechanical methods of timekeeping, many plants and animals, including humans, responded to cycles in the environment for mating, breeding, feeding, sleeping, hibernating, migrating and navigation. In this chapter we will look at biological clocks and discuss the links between time and navigation – animal and human.

Biological Clocks

Jean-Jacques d'Ortous de Mairan was a French astronomer, but one of his most remarkable discoveries was in biology. In 1729 he discovered that certain plants showed daily leaf movements, upwards and downwards, which were synchronized to the cycles of light and darkness, but persisted if the plant was placed in continuous dark. This was one of the first discoveries in the field of biological clocks. One of de Mairan's papers on the subject ended with the words,

'The progress of true science, which is the experimental kind, is necessarily slow.'

Despite slow progress in systematic research, many people were aware of the response of certain plants to the daily cycle. Carl Linnaeus, the eighteenth-century botanist, made use of the basic principle to construct a flower clock. Such clocks, which were not uncommon in the formal gardens of Europe in the eighteenth and nineteenth centuries, consisted of a number of flower-beds, each containing a different type of flower, which was chosen according to the time of day at which it opened or closed. For example: the spotted cat's ear opens at 6 a.m., the African marigold opens at 7 a.m., the star of Bethlehem opens at 11 a.m., the scarlet pimpernel closes at 2 p.m. and the evening primrose opens at 6 p.m. It was thus possible to tell the time by noting which flowers were open and which were closed, to an accuracy of about one hour.

Many plants and animals follow roughly twenty-four-hour rhythms, which are normally termed circadian rhythms. This term was first coined by Franz Halberg, a cancer specialist working at the University of Minnesota Medical School, who combined *circa*, meaning about, and *dian*, an early morning trumpet call or drum roll. Just as many industrial plants work a shift system to maximize the available resources, so many animals work on different 'shifts' in order to maximize the use of habitable niches of the environment. Among those that work the day shift are many birds, butterflies, honey-bees and lizards. Bats, owls, moths, mice and cockroaches are just a few examples of those that work the night shift. Green plants use sunlight during the day in the process of photosynthesis, and during the night they are involved in the processes of assimilation and growth. Many plants, for example the bean seedlings with which de Mairan made his discovery, follow daily sleep rhythms, raising their leaves by day and allowing them to droop at night. Some plants synchronize the opening of their blossoms with the activity rhythms of the animals that pollinate them.

The plants and animals of the seashore often follow cycles that are synchronized to the ebb and flow of the tides. There are two high tides (and two low tides) per day, and the interval between the high tides is about 12 hours 25 minutes. Barnacles, clams, snails and oysters are active when submerged by the incoming tide, whereas the fiddler crab and many shore birds feed on the living organisms that are exposed by the ebb tide. Some of the animals of the intertidal zone have two sets of rhythms; one following the tide and one following the solar day. For example, the fiddler crab has an activity rhythm synchronized with the times of the local tides, and a daily rhythm of skin-colour change. Since the lunar day is 24 hours 50 minutes, it means that the two rhythms of the fiddler crab will synchronize at two tides during a lunar month and these two tides will be separated by about a fortnight.

Lunar-annual Changes and Solar-annual Changes

We are all aware of annual changes in plant and animal life. The keen gardener must understand and use these annual changes if he is to make a success of gardening. We also know that migratory birds appear and disappear at specific times of the year, and that some animals hibernate in the winter. Indeed it was this realization that led early cultures to an interest in calendar-making and astronomy. Perhaps less well known are the cycles followed by some animals in which use is made of either combined daily and annual changes, or combined tidal and annual changes.

An example of a combined daily–annual rhythm is shown by migratory birds. Many migratory birds rapidly increase their weight before they start their long flights, building up large deposits of fat which they use as food reserves *en route*. These fat deposits are laid down in spring, within about ten days, and there is another period of migratory fattening in the late summer, but the rate of gain is slower than in the spring. Experiments have shown that the start of these periods is controlled by the changes in the length of the day which accompany the seasons. These experiments took the form of exposing the birds to light for periods that varied in a similar way to the annual changes in the length of the day. Another activity of migratory birds that is controlled by changes in the length of the day is the nocturnal restlessness – known as the *Zugunruhe* – that they display shortly before they set off on their migratory flights.

The palolo sea worms of the South Pacific provide an excellent example of a tidal–annual cycle. These worms are about eighteen inches long and normally live in dim caverns of the South Pacific. The main sex cycle of these worms occurs once a year, during the last quarter of the Moon in November, which corresponds to spring in the south. Details of the behaviour of the palolo were noted by

William Burrows, who was a commissioner on one of the islands in the 1940s. He noted that there were normally two risings, when these worms swarm on to the beaches in large numbers: a small one in October, and a larger one in November. He also recorded that the 'main rising always occurs at dawn, and literally, the worm comes up with the sun. It is, also, always at the time of high water.' The swarming of the palolo thus represents a fairly complex type of cycle. It occurs during a specific month of the year (November), it occurs at the last quarter of the Moon, at dawn and at high tide.

Animal Navigators

Very closely allied to biological clocks are the methods of navigation used by animal navigators. Several different investigations have shown that those birds that migrate during the day can use the Sun as a navigational aid. This implies that they are using their internal clocks to adjust the direction in which they are flying with respect to the Sun. If they are flying south, then in the early morning they must have the Sun on their left, at midday they must have the Sun directly ahead of them, and in the afternoon the Sun must be on their right. This hypothesis has been tested using the following experiment. Some birds were placed in artificial daylight conditions, in which the times of sunrise and sunset were changed by a specific number of hours. This had the effect of resetting their internal clocks by the same number of hours. When released under the real sky the birds flew in the wrong direction by the number of degrees the Sun would have moved in that time. These experiments provided strong support for this theory.

Bees also use the Sun as a compass, but instead of using the actual direction of the Sun, they use the polarization of the sky which is associated with the direction of the Sun. The light from the sky near the zenith, on a clear day, is polarized at right angles to the direction of the Sun (i.e. the light waves are vibrating at right angles to the direction of the Sun), and this polarization can be detected by the complex eyes of bees. Since the polarization of the sky depends on the direction of the Sun with respect to the compass directions, it means that the bees must be finding direction by using their ability to detect polarization in conjunction with their internal biological clocks. This important discovery was made by Karl von Frisch, who is well known for his studies of the social life of bees.

Birds that migrate at night seem to use the stars as a navigational aid. There have been several different investigations which support this idea. The first comes directly from observations in the field. Birds released under clear skies tend to fly in definite compass directions, whereas birds released under overcast skies fly in random directions. In another experiment one group of birds was fitted with contact lenses which allowed them to see objects under normal daylight conditions, but obscured starlight, while a second control group were not fitted with these lenses. When released under the night sky the birds in the first group took longer to find their way home than those of the second group. In a repeat of this experiment the birds were divided into three groups. The first group were fitted with contact lenses and had small magnets tied to their feet (to swamp any effect of the Earth's magnetic field), the second group were fitted with contact lenses only, while the last group had neither contact lenses or magnets. The birds of the first group never returned home, while those in the second group took longer to reach home than those of the last group. This seems to indicate that birds can navigate either by the stars or by the magnetic field of the Earth, although they seem to use the stars by preference. Further experiments under the simulated night sky of a planetarium seem to confirm this. Normally when birds are placed in cylindrical cages, under a real clear sky, just before they start their migratory flights, they tend to hop in the direction in which they will eventually fly. Under the artificial sky of the planetarium they tend to do the same thing. Does this mean that they can actually identify constellations and hence find the Pole Star? This does not seem to be the case. The planetarium experiment was repeated with the sky moving about a different 'Pole Star'. The birds then took their directional cue from this new 'Pole Star'. This seems to suggest that the birds might be using the movements of the sky rather than recognizable patterns of stars.

Human Rhythms

This is such a wide-ranging subject that we will just restrict ourselves to a brief mention of a few typical examples. Experiments by A. Jores and J. Frees showed that there exists a daily cycle in the tolerance of humans to pain, at least as far as the skin and teeth are concerned.

Between the hours of 8 p.m. and 8 a.m. the teeth are much less sensitive to painful stimulus than they are at other times of the day. The sensitivity to pain reaches a maximum at about 6 p.m. There also exists a daily rhythm in the metabolism of alcohol in the body. Between 2 p.m. and midnight, alcohol is burned more quickly than at other times of the day.

An important set of results on human rhythms was obtained from a series of experiments carried out by potholers, who spent periods in isolation, in caves, ranging from eight to twenty-five weeks. These potholers, under conditions of isolation, developed sleep–wakefulness rhythms which were all longer than 24 hours, with the average being 24 hours 42 minutes. In order to repeat and extend this type of work under more controlled laboratory conditions, an isolation facility was specially built at the Max Planck Institute for Physiology of Behaviour near Munich. Using this facility – called the *Tier Bunker* (*Tier* being the German for 'animal') – J. Aschoff made a number of interesting discoveries. He investigated several different human rhythms, including body-temperature, sleep–wakefulness cycles, total urine volume and the excretory products calcium and potassium. Aschoff found that all these parameters and functions followed rhythmic cycles, but their periods were not necessarily related to each other, nor were they related to the solar day. Another investigation, by N. Kleitman and W. Engelmann, on the sleep rhythms of infants, showed that after three to six weeks their sleep–wakefulness rhythms were still rather erratic. However, by about the twenty-third to the twenty-sixth week there existed a definite period of sleep between 8 p.m. and 8 a.m.

There are also daily rhythms in our ability to perform simple tasks. For example, the ability to estimate an interval of sixty seconds varied with the time of day. Between 7 a.m. and 1 p.m. there was a tendency to underestimate the interval, whereas there was a tendency to overestimate the period between 1 p.m. and 8 p.m. At 7 a.m., 1 p.m. and 8 p.m. the estimates were very close to 60 seconds. A comparison between this and the body-temperature curve shows that the two are related. This was further borne out by an investigation of interval estimation on patients displaying non–normal temperature variations. The estimation ability decreases as the body temperature rises above the normal value. Other abilities that are related to body temperature are card dealing and sorting speeds, and the speed and accuracy with which people can carry out simple calculations. M. Blake made a comparison of the daily temperature variation of two groups of people, one consisting of introverts and one of extroverts. The results from the two groups show that the body temperature of introverts rose earlier in the morning, reached a maximum sooner, and fell earlier at night than that of the extroverts. Here we have an indication that some human rhythms may be related to personality traits. Is there any evidence that personality traits may be related to the time and date of birth? In other words, what is the evidence in favour of the claims of astrology? We will discuss this evidence very briefly in the last section of this chapter, and in much more detail in the next part of the book.

Human Navigation

In order to find their way across the trackless sea, seamen needed to know not only their direction (which could be found by means of a magnetic compass, or from the Sun and stars), but also their latitude and longitude. Latitude is the angular measure of distance north or south of the equator, and longitude is the measure of angular distance east or west of a given meridian – which since 1884 has been chosen as the Greenwich meridian. As the Earth spins on its own axis with respect to the Sun at the rate of fifteen degrees per hour, the time difference between two places, which differ by fifteen degrees of longitude, will be one hour. This is the basis of the time-zone system which envelops the world, formed by a system of lines of longitude running from north to south. These lines of longitude can be used to tell us how far east or west of the Greenwich meridian we are, provided we have means, such as radio, of comparing our local time with the time at Greenwich. This basic idea was used to develop a completely artificial method of position-fixing at sea.

Some years ago, before artificial satellites could be used for the purpose, a system of navigation was invented which made use of radio waves emitted by a series of radio transmitters placed at suitable points on land. Radio waves consist of a uniformly spaced series of peaks and troughs of electric field, and these radiated out in the form of concentric circles with the transmitter as their centre. With more than two transmitters broadcasting their waves in a synchronized way, the peaks from one transmitter will cancel out the troughs from the other at certain points in the region surrounding the transmitters, and at other points the peaks (or the troughs) will reinforce each other. This means that a pattern, called an interference pattern, will be set up around the transmitter. A special receiver on board a ship can monitor this pattern, and with the aid of maps showing the position of the transmitters and giving a diagrammatic view of the interference pattern, a navigator can translate this information into fixing his position at sea. Thus we see that two wave trains, emitted as a sequence of peaks and troughs in time and synchronized in time, can yield, if interpreted in the appropriate manner, information on our location in space. This general principle is also at the basis of the new satellite method of navigation. A series of synchronized time impulses is emitted from radio transmitters on board a number of satellites circling the globe. These impulses can be picked up by a special receiver on board a ship or plane. Each satellite is a different distance from the craft, and so the transmitted impulses will have different distances to travel, and hence will take different times to reach the observer. A minicomputer attached to the receiver can translate these time differences into positional information, which gives the navigator his position at sea.

The Nature of the Biological Clock

The general subject of biological clocks raises the question about whether the clocks are direct responses to the environment or of internal origin. Most experiments show that many of the rhythms discussed above will persist even after the organism is shielded from the external stimulus with which it is apparently synchronized, but if the organism is removed from its own environment for a long period of time the various parts which exhibit rhythms become desynchronized. The results of these experiments seem to suggest that most organisms possess fairly stable internal timers, which do not always correspond exactly with associated astronomical cycles, but that these internal timers have to be occasionally adjusted by external geophysical periods. This is rather like resetting one's own clocks and watches using the radio time pips. It seems very likely, then, that the processes of evolution gave selective advantages to those individuals that had internal timers with periods very close to those of the physical environment of our Earth.

This point was well made by J. L. Cloudsley-Thompson in his book *Biological Clocks*:

In so far as all biological clocks are part and parcel of their evolving rhythmic environment, a good case can be made in support of the idea that biological clocks are both endogenous (of internal origin) and exogenous, but to different extents. Although the physiological clock may be endogenous in the usually accepted sense, it cannot be divorced from its genetic ancestry, which has been influenced by natural selection. Thus the rhythms of plants and animals must have arisen, in an evolutionary context, from cellular phenomena which have subsequently been strengthened by natural selection.

One well-known researcher in the field of biological clocks was the late Professor Frank Brown. His experiments on the tidal rhythms of some marine animals showed that light was not the only environmental cue used for the resetting of the internal biological clock, and that in this and in other cases one cycle was insufficient to reset the clock. After a lifetime of research in this area of biology, Brown was led to the conclusion that many different subtle geophysical factors, including cyclical changes of the geomagnetic field, could be used by a variety of animals to reset their internal biological clocks.

Biological Clocks and the Geomagnetic Field

Some of Brown's experiments, on a wide range of living organisms, showed that the ability of many different animals to know the times of the tides, the time of day, the phases of the Moon and the time of year, could not all be explained in terms of light cues. He was able to demonstrate that the geomagnetic field in general, and its cyclical fluctuations in particular, could influence the biological clocks and internal compasses of many different species of animals. Experiments carried out by Professor James Gould, mainly on birds and bees, led him to suggest that the magnetic field of our Earth was second only to the Sun and sky in helping animals to know the time, their location and direction.

Dr Robert Becker suggested a mechanism for this interaction between the geomagnetic field and life. Starting with the well-known fact that there are electrical–potential differences between the various parts of a living body, he went on to suggest that this potential was an important controlling factor in the activities of the body. He further suggested that this potential system was frequency-sensitive, responding to certain frequencies and not to others. He concluded that over the aeons the biological clocks of every living organism had, in a sense, become phase-locked to specific pulsations of the geomagnetic field, since all life had evolved in this field.

Biological Pendulum Clocks

The endogenous and exogenous nature of biological clocks can be reconciled in a pendulum model of the clock. The rate at which a pendulum swings is determined by its length. Once the pendulum is set in motion, by a single push, it will continue to swing at a constant rate, but its amplitude will decrease, because it is losing energy all the time through friction with the air and in its bearings. In order to keep it swinging, energy has to be fed into the system at frequent intervals, which are either equal to the period, or suitable multiples of this period. The amount of energy which has to be imparted on each cycle will depend on its friction with the air and on its bearings. This is usually referred to as the damping of the system. It is this damping that will cause the pendulum to stop oscillating after a certain length of time, if the feeding of energy into the system is stopped at a particular moment. The larger the amount of damping, the more quickly the pendulum will stop. If there is no damping at all then, in principle, the pendulum will oscillate for ever, once it has been set in motion, even if no other energy is subsequently fed into the system. No damping also means that only energy fed in with exactly the natural frequency of the pendulum will be accepted, and energy fed in at any other frequency will be ignored. It also means that energy fed into the system at this frequency will be 'remembered', and the amplitude of the oscillations will continue to increase until the supply of energy is stopped.

Damping has advantages and disadvantages. We have already seen that it will cause the amplitude to decay if no energy is fed into the system at appropriate frequencies, so this is a disadvantage. However, damping also means that energy fed in within a certain narrow range on either side of the natural frequency can also keep the pendulum swinging. This range is called the bandwidth of the pendulum. This increases with the amount of damping. We can use these ideas as a model for understanding the behaviour of biological clocks.

Evolutionary selection determines the 'length' of the pendulum in such a way that its natural period of oscillation is matched to the average period of a natural cycle, like, for example, the length of the day or the time between two high tides. The observed fact that in a laboratory biological clocks can go on for several cycles without exposure to obvious rhythmic cues in the environment, means that the damping in these clocks is relatively small. This means that the bandwidth is also small, and so the range of periods at which it will accept and 'remember' energy supplied to it will be narrow. In biological terms this means that these clocks can only be entrained by frequencies very close to the natural frequency of the system, and not by other frequencies. The number of external cycles needed to restart the natural oscillations, once they have died out, will also depend on the damping of the system and the amount of energy imparted during each cycle. If the amount of energy fed in during one cycle is large, then one cycle may be sufficient to restart the natural oscillations of the system. If the light cycle of day and night is the principal entraining mechanism of a particular clock, then, because the amount of energy imparted by each cycle is large, one cycle is sufficient to entrain the clock. The work of Frank Brown suggests that other rhythmic cues in the environment can act as entrainers of the clock, but because the amount of energy fed in by these cues may be considerably less than the photoperiodic cue of day and night, more cycles are usually necessary to entrain a clock when it has been removed from access to sunlight. In the case of solar-day rhythms, the alternative entraining cues might be daily changes in atmospheric pressure, or they might be the cyclical vibrations of the Earth's magnetic field, which are called the solar daily magnetic variation. In the case of clocks normally entrained by the varying height of water on a beach due to the tides, alternative cues might be the lunar tides in the atmosphere, or the lunar daily magnetic variation, if the organism possessing the clock is removed from the beach. The pendulum model is thus a very powerful model which enables us to understand the basic operation of biological clocks.

In this chapter we have seen that all living organisms have extension not only in space but also in time. The sense of time of many organisms can be used as a navigational aid, and thus it can help them to explore other parts of their environment, and in doing so it helps them to extend their personal experience of space beyond the space accessible to their senses. Evolutionary selection has synchronized many biological clocks to environmental cycles like day and night, the tides and the seasons. These cycles are themselves a result of the time-dependent orientation and motions of the Earth in space, so biological clocks are inherited memories of the Earth's journey through space and time.

4 | The Observer and the Universe

> There was a Door to which I found no Key:
> There was a Veil past which I could not see:
> Some little Talk awhile of ME and THEE
> There seem'd – and then no more of THEE and ME.
>
> Edward Fitzgerald, *The Rubáiyát of Omar Khayyám*

Now and again we hear people refer to the two cultures of our society – the arts on the one hand and the sciences on the other hand. Quite often it is implied that there is a great gulf between the two groups of disciplines. Although this is true, in some sense, in the languages used and the methods employed by the arts and the sciences to discuss and present their results, there are very great similarities in the world views of the artist and the scientist, and in their underlying methodology. This has become apparent in our own century as a result of advances in physical theories concerning the relationship between the observer and the observed.

Robert Hughes's book *The Shock of the New* is subtitled 'Art and the Century of Change', and in it he explores developments in twentieth-century art and design, and their relationship to changes in society and science. At one point he says:

The idea that the looker affects the sight is taken for granted in most fields of scientific inquiry today ... In the late nineteenth century, this was not generally thought to be true ... Nevertheless, towards 1900, as one sees the idea developing in its scientific form in the work of F. H. Bradley, Alfred North Whitehead and Albert Einstein, so one artist, scientifically illiterate, ignorant of their work ... was labouring to explore it, give it aesthetic form and finally to base his work on it. His name was Paul Cézanne.

In this extract he is referring specifically to the idea of relativity. In the following extract he also introduces another concept important to twentieth-century physics – the concept of 'uncertainty':

But with Cézanne ... the statement, 'This is what I see', is replaced by a question, 'Is this what I see?' You share his hesitations about the position of a tree or a branch; or the final shape of Mont Ste-Victoire, and the tree in front of it. Relativity is all. Doubt becomes part of the painting's subject. Indeed, the idea that doubt can be heroic, if it is locked into a structure as grand as that of the paintings of Cézanne's old age, is one of the keys to our century, a touchstone of modernity itself.

The importance of uncertainty, and its relationship to art, is also mentioned by the scientist, Dr Jacob Bronowski, in his book *The Ascent of Man*. At the start of his chapter on 'Knowledge and Certainty' he says:

One aim of the physical sciences has been to give an exact picture of the material world. One achievement of physics in the twentieth century has been to prove that that aim is unattainable.

In the television series that accompanied the book, he introduced the idea of uncertainty by referring to a portrait of Stephen Borgrajewicz, painted by the Polish artist, Feliks Topolski, in the following terms:

In the portrait . . . we are aware that such a picture does not so much fix the face as explore it: that the artist is tracing the detail almost as if by touch; and that each line that is added strengthens the picture but never makes it final. We accept that as the method of the artist.

   But what physics has now done is to show that that is the only method of knowledge. There is no absolute knowledge. And those who claim it, whether they are scientists or dogmatists, open the door to tragedy. All information is imperfect. We have to treat it with humility. That is the human condition; and that is what quantum physics says. I mean that literally.

In this chapter we will explore some of the basic ideas of Einstein's theories of relativity and the quantum theory.

The Need for a Theory of Relativity

In the introduction we briefly mentioned the Michelson–Morley experiment, which Lord Kelvin saw as one of the 'clouds' on the horizon of physics at the turn of the century. The physicists of the nineteenth century believed that electromagnetic radiation propagated through a medium called the ether, in a way not dissimilar to the propagation of sound waves through air. The Michelson–Morley experiment was an attempt to measure the speed of the Earth through this ether, which physicists believed was at rest with respect to the 'framework' of the universe.

The idea of this experiment can be understood by first of all considering the progress of two swimmers. The first swimmer swims across a river whose water is all moving at the same speed, and back. Since he wishes to cross the river at right angles, he can only do so by heading upstream in each case, so as to allow for the fact that the river will tend to carry him downstream. The other swimmer, who swims at exactly the same speed as the first, swims the same total distance as the first, but he goes upstream and then downstream, rather than trying to cross the river. If one works out the times it takes the two swimmers to complete their round trips it turns out that they are different. Michelson used this principle to try to measure the speed of the earth through the ether.

His two 'swimmers' were beams of light, from a single source, split into two beams of identical path length. The 'river' was the ether, which, from the point of view of a piece of apparatus attached to the Earth, would seem to flow past the equipment. One beam travelled parallel to the direction of the Earth in its orbit, the other perpendicular to this direction. The light from the two beams was combined to produce an interference pattern. In 1887 Albert Michelson built a device based on this principle – called an interferometer. With the assistance of Edward Morley, he then set out to find the speed of the Earth. They reasoned that there should be a time delay between the two beams which would be different for two different orientations of the interferometer – one position being the 'normal' position described above, and one with the interferometer rotated through ninety degrees. This difference could be detected, they assumed, by a shift in the interference pattern produced by combining the two beams. They found no such shift, which seemed, at first, to indicate that the Earth was at rest with respect to the ether!

In 1892 the Dutch physicist Hendrik Lorentz offered another explanation for the negative result of the Michelson–Morley experiment. He assumed that the forces holding molecules together were electromagnetic in origin, and they were therefore propagated through the ether. If this was the case, then the particles of which a body was composed, moving through the stationary field represented by the ether, would be pushed together parallel to the line of motion. Hence the arm of the interferometer parallel to the Earth's motion shortens slightly with respect to the other. Lorentz was able to show that the amount of shortening was precisely that needed to cancel out the effect of motion through the ether expected from Maxwell's theory. An Irish physicist, George Fitzgerald, put forward a similar explanation to explain the failure of the experiment to detect the Earth's motion through the ether. Although it is not clear if Einstein was aware of the experiment, or these explanations, his special theory of relativity was able to explain the result obtained by Michelson and Morley. Einstein was able to demonstrate that the measurement of length and time by observers travelling at different speeds, and in different directions, depended on their relative speeds and directions. This meant that the distance travelled by a light beam in the direction of the Earth's motion would appear to be different, to an observer on the Earth, to the distance travelled by a beam of light at right angles to the Earth's motion. Besides its other consequences, Einstein's work showed that there was no need to postulate the existence of the mysterious ether.

The Special Theory of Relativity

The laws that govern our day-to-day lives, our interactions with other people, our births, our marriages and our deaths, will, of course, vary, depending on the country in which we are living, because they are human laws, constructed by people for the smooth running of societies with given sets of values. The laws of physics are rather different in character. They should not depend on where they are discovered, or on the locations in which they are applied or tested. They are required to be valid throughout the observable universe.

The concept of the universality of the laws of physics is relatively recent in the history of science, and it can be traced back to Newton's formulation of the laws of motion and the law of gravitation. In Aristotle's cosmology the laws of physics were not universal. There were two distinct sets of laws, one for the superlunar sphere, the region beyond the Moon, and one for the sublunar sphere, the region below the Moon. Kepler's laws of motion were the traffic rules for the planets – they did not apply to the motion of objects on the surface of the Earth. Newton made an important discovery concerning the character of physical laws – they must be valid no matter where we apply them in the universe.

Einstein discovered another characteristic of the laws of physics, which he used as a basic concept of the special theory of relativity: they had to be true for all observers that were moving at constant speeds in straight lines with respect to each other. In other words, the mathematical formulae used to describe the laws of physics had to be independent of the motion of the observers – provided they were travelling at constant speeds in straight lines. If one were to test these laws in a laboratory at rest on the surface of Earth, in a train, or a spacecraft, moving along in a straight line at constant speed, or at the bottom of a mine, one should always find these laws to be true.

The other basic principle of Einstein's special theory of relativity was that the speed of light was the same throughout the universe, and it did not depend on the speed with which the observer was moving. The application of these basic principles to the known laws of physics had many far-reaching consequences. The special theory required that the length of a measuring rod would be different for observers moving at different speeds. Thus, for example, the length of a spacecraft as measured by an astronaut working outside the craft, would be different from its length as measured by means of a telescope fixed to the Earth. If the spacecraft was moving close to the speed of light, then to the earthbound observer it would seem shorter than it was before it left the Earth, whereas the astronaut would find its length unchanged.

One can find the mass of an electron by the extent to which it is deflected in a magnetic field of known strength. If one measured the mass of an electron moving close to the speed of light, then it would be much more massive than the mass of an electron moving at a much slower speed. This result of the special theory has been verified over and over again in the enormous machines used to smash sub-atomic particles together. Another consequence of the theory is that from the point of view of an observer at rest, the clocks on board a spacecraft travelling close to the speed of light would seem to have slowed up, whereas no change would be detected by astronauts on board the craft. All these results of the special theory are particularly important for subatomic physicists working on fast-moving particles and for astronomers making observations on distant galaxies that are receding from us at very high speeds.

Mass, Energy and the Speed of Light

We have already seen that the special theory requires that the mass of a particle will increase as it gets close to the speed of light. The equations of relativity tell us that at the speed of light a particle will have infinite mass, so this means that there is not enough energy in the universe to give any particle this speed, and hence no particle can travel faster than light. The theory also leads to the conclusion that if a small amount of mass is destroyed, then it will be manifested as energy. It also tells us that any localization of energy has mass.

When four hydrogen atoms are forced, by the high temperatures within the stars, to combine with each other to form one helium atom, then there is some mass lost. It is this loss of mass which manifests itself as energy, and it is this energy that provides the fuel for most ordinary stars. The transmission of information normally requires the transfer of energy, and since energy has mass, it means that no information can be transmitted faster than light. This means that the speed of light is the speed limit for matter and information in normal space.

Relativity and the Michelson–Morley Experiment

The special theory of relativity explains the negative result obtained in the Michelson–Morley experiment. The theory shows that the lengths of two equal measuring rods moving at different speeds in the same direction will appear to be different if both rods are aligned along the direction of motion, but their lengths will appear the same if the rods are both at right angles to the direction of motion. Thus the theory, by clarifying our concepts of measurement, is able to explain why there is a difference in the measurement of the lengths which the two light beams in the Michelson–Morley experiment have to traverse, without requiring the physical change of length suggested by Lorentz and Fitzgerald.

World Lines in Space and Time

The special theory of relativity is most eloquently represented in the space-time continuum, which consists of three dimensions of space and one of time. It is extremely difficult to imagine a four-dimensional space, but we can use analogies to illustrate the basic ideas, and in many cases it is not always necessary to consider all the dimensions of space.

The position of a ship can be given in terms of its latitude and longitude at a given time. Imagine plotting its position on a chart drawn on a sheet of transparent perspex at a given time, and its position at a later time on another sheet. Consider plotting its position every hour on a series of sheets, and then stacking these sheets on top of each other, in sequence, separating each sheet from the next by means of perspex blocks placed at the corners. If instead of just plotting the positions at subsequent times, we had actually drilled a small hole in each sheet, then we could have threaded a bit of cotton through each hole, and the thread would have represented the progress of the ship over the surface of our Earth, as well as its progress through time. This thread represents the world line of the ship through space-time. Even an object at rest has a world line, but in this case the world line would be moving only through time – it would be a vertical line through our sheets of perspex.

The orbit of a planet around the Sun is really an ellipse, but for most planets the orbits are more like circles to a very high degree of accuracy. However, the world line of a planet in space-time would be like a spiral, because the planet is not only orbiting the Sun, it is also progressing through time. Each and every particle in the universe has a world line in space-time, but the shapes of these world lines vary a great deal. The world lines of two particles that have collided with each other will intersect at the point of space and at the time at which they collided. Particles that have been at the same point in space, but at different times, will not intersect.

The General Theory of Relativity

Newton's law of gravitation does not fit into Einstein's special theory of relativity. One reason for this is that it requires instantaneous action at a distance, and this is in conflict with the requirement of special relativity that no information can be transmitted at a speed faster than the speed of light. Einstein's attempts to formulate a new theory led him to the general theory of relativity, which is really a theory of gravitation.

There are two basic principles to the general theory. The first is a statement concerning, once again, the character of the laws of physics. The theory requires that the laws should be stated in such a way that they do not depend on where the laws are applied, and they do not depend on how the observer is moving. This means that its requirements are more general than those of the special theory, which require the laws to be true for observers travelling at constant speeds in straight lines with respect to each other. The results of the special theory are strictly not valid when one is close to a strong gravitational field, or if one is changing one's direction of motion, or if one is changing the speed at which one is moving. The results of the special theory have to be replaced by those of the general theory in these cases.

The second basic principle is called the principle of equivalence. This principle asserts that gravitation and acceleration have a great deal in common, and that they are, in a sense, equivalent. We have all had some experience of this assertion. When a lift first starts to accelerate upwards we feel a slight increase in our weight, and a sinking feeling in our stomachs. When the lift stops we feel a slight feeling of weightlessness. This means that we can increase the force of gravitation on our bodies by accelerating upwards, and we can decrease the force of gravitation by accelerating downwards. We can also experience gravitation-like forces when we are sitting in a car that is accelerating very rapidly. In this case we are pressed back against the seat by the resulting force. Astronauts are most aware of these G-forces when they are accelerating upwards in their spacecraft. In order to learn to cope with these forces they are trained in a centrifuge, which in effect simulates these G-forces.

World Lines in General Relativity

These two basic ideas lead to several conclusions of far-reaching importance. The first concerns the motion of particles. According to Newton's first law of motion, a particle will continue its state of rest, or its motion in a straight line at a constant speed, unless it is acted on by a force which will tend to change either of these initial states. This means that rest or motion at constant speed in a straight line are the normal conditions of particles, and if they are in one or other of these two states, then we know that no forces are acting on them.

Under either of these two possible states the world line of a particle in space-time would just be a straight line.

The mathematical definition of a straight line is that it is the shortest distance between two points. This is true if we are joining two points on a plane surface or in ordinary three-dimensional space, but it is not true if we are limited to moving on a curved surface or within a confined region of space that has curvature. For boats and ships travelling on the surface of the sea, which is curved, the curvature has to be taken into account when planning a route. An aircraft is confined to the atmosphere of Earth, the altitude of which is small in comparison with the radius of the Earth, so once again we have to take into account the curvature of the atmosphere when flying over large distances. Pilots and the navigators of ships are very aware of this. In going from one port to another distant port a few thousand miles away, seamen know that they have to sail along what are called arcs of great circles – a great circle being one which cuts the surface of Earth exactly in half. Such a circle is a special case of a class of mathematical curves which are called geodesics, and they represent the 'shortest distance' between two points on a curved surface or in 'curved' space. We can use this concept to discuss one of the consequences of the general theory.

The general theory sees motion under gravity as being 'normal' motion, so we do not have to look for other forces unless a body is moving differently from its 'normal motion'. However, its world line through space and time will only be straight if it is a long way from any massive object. According to this theory the 'shape' of space-time near massive objects is not flat but curved, and therefore under the conditions of a 'curved' space-time particles will follow special curved paths which will be geodesics. The 'curvature' of space-time is determined by the presence and distribution of matter, and since energy also has mass, it is also determined by the distribution of energy. The rules that allow us to calculate the curvature of space-time from the distribution of mass and energy are called the field equations.

Once we have calculated the curvature of space-time, using these field equations, we can calculate the geodesics of this space-time, and these will tell us how particles will move if they are subjected to no other forces, such as, for example, electricity and magnetism. A ray of light will, because information travels along it at the speed of light, be a special type of geodesic, called a 'null-geodesic'. Far away from all massive objects, this null-geodesic will be a straight line. This means that over the vast distances between stars, we can treat light as if it is travelling in straight lines, to a high degree of approximation. This is no longer true near massive objects.

Near the Earth, which is less massive than the Sun, the curvature of the light beam is slight. However, the effect on a ray of light just grazing the surface of the Sun can be detected, in the appropriate circumstances. Such a situation arises during a total eclipse of the Sun. Suppose that at a given time of year, a particular star is just behind the Sun, so that some of the rays of light from this star would just graze its surface, and then reach the surface of Earth. In effect we will be able to see just behind the Sun. Under normal circumstances the brightness of the Sun would prevent us from seeing the star, but during a total eclipse of the Sun, the Moon will come between us and the Sun, thus blotting out its rays, and so we will be able to see the star. Because the Moon is much less massive than the Sun, its own effect will be negligible. The first time this experiment was carried out was on the occasion of an eclipse that took place in 1919. When the photographic observations taken during this eclipse were worked out, they provided convincing confirmation of the predictions of the general theory of relativity, and Albert Einstein became an internationally famous scientist almost overnight.

Quantum Theory

The Origins of the Quantum Theory

Quantum theory had its origins in the work of Max Planck, a German physicist, who presented an important paper on the subject in 1900. Planck was trying to explain the shape of the black-body spectrum. We are all familiar with such phrases as 'red hot' or 'white hot', which emphasize the relationship between the colour of the light emitted by an object and its temperature. Objects that are 'white hot' are much hotter than objects that are 'red hot'. Most bodies 'broadcast' energy in a wide range of wavelengths, from X-rays to very long radio waves. However, at a given temperature most of the radiation given off will be close to a specific wavelength; that is, there is a specific relationship between the wavelength at which most of the radiation is emitted and the temperature. This relationship was first discovered by the German physicist Wilhelm Wien, so it is called Wien's law. It tells us that the wavelength at which most of the radiation is emitted gets shorter as the temperature of the body increases, so, since red light is of a longer wavelength than blue light, an object that emits red light will be cooler, relatively speaking, than one that emits blue light. Cooler objects will emit most of their radiation in the infra-red part of the spectrum, which our eyes cannot see. Objects which are cooler still will emit most of the radiation as very long radio waves. A very important feature of these results is that they do not depend on the material of which the objects are made.

The general shape of the curve which relates energy emitted to wavelength is called the black-body spectrum. Before Planck did his research physicists had been unable to understand the theoretical reasons for the shape of this curve. It was assumed that the energy carried by the radiation of a given wavelength could have any value, that is that the amount of energy carried could vary in a continuous way. What Planck did was to propose that radiation energy had to be discrete – that the energy had to come in little packets, and the size of the smallest packet depended on the wavelength, the speed of light and a constant, called Planck's constant. Such a packet of energy was called a quantum of radiation, and collections of such packets were called quanta. Using the concept of quanta, Planck was able to work out the shape of the black-body radiation curve, and so we now call this curve simply the Planck curve.

Einstein and the Quantum Theory

There was another problem that existed in physics at the turn of the century. It involved a phenomenon called the photoelectric effect. When light strikes the surfaces of certain metals, in a vacuum, it was observed that electrons could be ejected from the surface. This could not be explained if the energy carried by light varied continuously. Einstein saw the importance of Planck's quanta for explaining this phenomenon. If one assumed that the little packets of light energy behaved as if they were particles, then a 'particle' or 'quantum' of light could collide with an electron near the surface of the metal and as a result the electron would be emitted from the surface. The photoelectric effect is the basic principle behind television and video cameras and light meters.

Quantum Theory and the Bohr Atom

The Danish physicist, Niels Bohr, successfully applied quantum theory to exploring the structure of the atom and the specific set of spectral lines emitted by atoms of different elements. In Chapter 2 we saw that Rutherford proposed a model for the atom in which a number of electrons orbited a central nucleus, which had a positive charge. According to Maxwell's classical theory of electromagnetism, the electrons doing this orbiting would be radiating electromagnetic waves continuously, and since this meant that they were losing energy, they would spiral into the central nucleus. Bohr applied quantum theory to the problem. By doing so he was able to show that the electrons in the hydrogen atom could only orbit the nucleus in certain 'allowed' orbits that were specific distances from the central nucleus. When an electron is orbiting in any one of these orbits, it does not radiate. However, it does give off radiation, of a definite wavelength, when it moves from an orbit far from the nucleus to one closer to the nucleus. In other words, it does not radiate while it is in a stable orbit, but it radiates when moving from one orbit to another. It could also absorb radiation of a definite wavelength, and move from an orbit close to the nucleus to one farther out. It is this behaviour of electrons that gives rise to the observed set of spectral lines which could be used to identify the atoms of different chemical elements.

De Broglie Waves and the Bohr Atom

Prince Louis de Broglie was a French nobleman who made an important contribution to early quantum theory. Just as Planck and Einstein had shown that light waves sometimes behaved as if they were made up of particles, so de Broglie proposed that particles could sometimes behave as if they were waves. In his paper de Broglie proposed, not that the particles sometimes 'turn into' waves, but that 'pilot' waves guided the motion of particles, and hence under certain circumstances they would demonstrate the type of behaviour that one normally associated with waves. These waves were not at all like electromagnetic waves, and they were sometimes referred to as 'matter waves'. De Broglie was also aware that these waves had to propagate through space faster than light. This was necessary because these pilot waves acted as if they were guiding the particle, 'informing' it where it had to go. Thus to get ahead of a particle travelling just slightly slower than the speed of light, these waves had to travel faster than light, in order to 'probe' the region of space ahead of it. An analogy may help to explain this. The navigator of a supersonic jet plane, flying at night, or in fog, has to use the radar of the aircraft (which uses radio waves travelling at the speed of light) to probe the space ahead of the plane. It is not possible to use sound waves for the same purpose, as bats do, because the plane is travelling faster than sound, and thus it would reach objects in front of it before sound waves emitted by the plane could return to inform the navigator of objects ahead of it.

De Broglie went on to point out that this did not conflict with the theory of relativity, because it was their 'phase velocity' that could be greater than light, whereas energy was transported at the group velocity, which was always less than the speed of light. The concepts of phase velocity and group velocity can easily be understood with reference to the expanding ring of waves that propagates outward when a stone is dropped into a pond. The ring itself will, on careful inspection, be seen to consist of a number of smaller wavelets which start on the inner edge, move through the ring, and decay on the outer edge. These wavelets seem to be moving faster than the ring as a whole. They are moving with their respective phase velocities, whereas the ring as a whole moves with the group velocity.

Schrödinger and the Structure of the Atom

The work of de Broglie in some ways represented a transition in the approaches to quantum theory. It gave rise to the work of Erwin Schrödinger, and this work in turn gave rise to a much more formal and mathematical approach to the application of quantum theory to physical problems. The contributions made by Planck, Einstein and de Broglie were based more on physical intuition than on mathematical sophistication. Schrödinger's work was to change all that.

It has been said that Schrödinger first heard about the work of de Broglie in a reference in one of Einstein's papers. He decided that it might be possible to improve on the Bohr model of the atom by taking the wave nature of the electron into account. The de Broglie wavelength associated with a moving electron depended, among other qualities, on its speed. Schrödinger was able to show that the Bohr orbits corresponded to speeds (which depended on the sizes of the orbits) that gave rise to wavelengths which would fit a whole number of times into the circumference of the orbits. Other orbits were not allowed because the associated wavelengths could not fit a whole number of times into the circumference.

All waves, from electromagnetic waves to water waves, are governed by a class of mathematical formulae called wave equations. Schrödinger generalized the work of de Broglie to derive such an equation, called the Schrödinger wave equation.

Further Developments in Quantum Mechanics

The German physicist Arnold Sommerfeld, in 1916, generalized the work of Bohr (which restricted the electron orbits in the atom to circular ones) to include elliptical orbits, and in doing so he had to include the results of Einstein's special theory of relativity. Schrödinger also tried to include relativity in the formulation of his equation, but at this stage it was not known that the electron also had spin – it behaved, in certain respects, as if it were spinning on its own axis, rather like a planet – which led to discrepancies in observations. He abandoned the attempt, and as a result his equation does not include relativity.

It was left to the British physicist Paul Dirac to succeed in including relativity in an equation which describes the motion of subatomic particles. This equation is naturally known as the Dirac equation, and it showed not only that the spin of the electron was a necessary consequence of the theory of relativity, but also that there should exist particles with the same mass as the electron, but with a positive charge. A particle having these properties was discovered two years later by the American physicist Carl Anderson, and this discovery was later confirmed by Patrick Blackett, a British physicist. This particle is now called the positron.

Werner Heisenberg, a German physicist, had followed a much

more mathematical approach to quantum theory, making use of matrices, and hence his version became known as matrix mechanics, whereas the Schrödinger version became known as wave mechanics. The two approaches were later shown to be equivalent. Heisenberg is probably best known for the formulation of the uncertainty principle which bears his name. According to this principle it is impossible to know both the position and the momentum (which is speed multiplied by mass) of a subatomic particle at the same time. If one makes an accurate measurement of the speed of a particle, then the act of measurement will make the measurement of its position very uncertain.

This concept can be understood by means of a simple analogy. A police radar speed trap works by bouncing radio waves off cars, and then measuring the change in wavelength that arises from the Doppler shift, which we discussed in Chapter 1. The momentum in the radio beam is small in comparison with the momentum of the car, so the bouncing of the beam off the car will only reduce its speed by an extremely small amount. In order to measure the speed of an electron, one would have to use very short electromagnetic waves, like, for example, X-rays, and the energy in the beam would have to be sufficient to change the position of the particle.

Quantum Mechanics and John von Neumann

John von Neumann was a mathematician of Hungarian origin who settled in America. An article in *Life* magazine said of him: 'The brilliant Hungarian mathematician who helped develop America's advanced electronic "brains" did not need them. He had one of the most prodigious minds ever seen in action.'

Von Neumann and Einstein both worked at the Institute of Advanced Studies in Princeton, and the article in *Life* quoted a member of the institute who had worked with both men: 'Einstein's mind was slow and contemplative. He would think about something for years. But Johnny's mind was lightning quick. He either solved a problem right away or not at all.'

In 1932 von Neumann wrote an important book entitled *The Mathematical Foundations of Quantum Mechanics*. In this book he placed quantum mechanics on a firm and sophisticated mathematical basis. In a section on 'Projections as Propositions', he said:

. . . the relationship between the properties of a physical system on the one hand, and the projections (wave function) on the other hand, makes possible a sort of logical calculus with these. However, in contrast to the concepts of ordinary logic, this system is extended by the concepts of 'simultaneous decidability' (the uncertainty principle) which is characteristic for quantum mechanics.

Von Neumann's work in quantum mechanics had some conceptual similarities with Einstein's work on relativity. Einstein had shown that the geometry of flat space-time, known as Euclidean geometry, was not universally valid over large cosmic distances and near massive objects. Von Neumann, and G. Birkhoff, had shown that classical logic was not universally valid, and that in quantum mechanics a new system of logic, called quantum logic, was necessary.

Many physicists, including Einstein, did not like the uncertainty of quantum mechanics, nor did they like the statistical interpretation that some physicists claimed should be given to the wave functions associated with quantum mechanics. Einstein is reputed to have said that he did not believe that '. . . God played dice with the universe'. It was their dissatisfaction with these aspects of quantum theory that led some physicists to propose that the theory could be made deterministic by the inclusion of 'hidden variables'. We will discuss this aspect of the subject, very briefly, in the next section.

Hidden Variables in Quantum Theory

Hidden variables have been defined as 'Any set of hypothetical physical quantities, knowledge of whose values would permit more precise predictions of the results of measurements on a system than the statistical predictions of quantum theory.' The normal statistical interpretation of quantum theory rules out the possibility of such hidden variables. John von Neumann produced a mathematical proof which was supposed to show conclusively that hidden variables were inconsistent with quantum mechanics. His standing in theoretical physics was such that this proof was taken as being the final word on the subject by most physicists, but not by all. In 1952 David Bohm showed that it was possible to understand the results of Schrödinger's non-realistic quantum mechanics by introducing a 'hidden variable' in the form of a 'quantum potential'. This 'quantum potential' had one surprising feature; like the pilot waves of Louis de Broglie, it had to propagate faster than light, because it carried information on the region ahead of the particle. In 1966 John Bell, a theoretical physicist from CERN in Geneva, proved a theorem, now called Bell's theorem, which shows that in quantum theory '. . . an explicit causal mechanism exists whereby the disposition of one piece of apparatus affects the results obtained with a distant piece'.

Bell's theorem demonstrates that if two particles have interacted in the past, then each particle carries a memory of that interaction which can be instantaneously recalled, so subsequent measurements on the pair will always be correlated. To quote from *The Cosmic Blueprint* by Paul Davies:

Bell showed that quantum mechanics predicts a significantly greater degree of correlation than can possibly be accounted for by any theory that treats the particles as independently real and subject to locality. It is as if the two particles engage in a conspiracy to cooperate when measurements are performed on them independently, even when these measurements are made simultaneously. The theory of relativity, however, forbids any sort of instant signalling or interaction to pass between the two particles. There seems to be a mystery, therefore, about how the conspiracy is established.

Gary Zukav in *The Dancing Wu Li Masters* summarizes very well the present implications regarding quantum logic and Bell's theorem:

Laser fusion research and the great quark hunt are endeavours within the existing paradigms of physics. A paradigm is an established thought process, a framework. Both quantum logic and Bell's theorem are potentially explosive in terms of existing frameworks. The first (quantum logic) calls us back from the realm of symbols to the realm of experience. The second (Bell's theorem) tells us that there is no such thing as 'separate parts'. All the 'parts' of the universe are connected in an intimate and immediate way previously claimed only by mystics and other scientifically objectionable people.

In this chapter we have looked at the two cornerstones of modern physics, the theories of relativity and quantum theory. We have also shown that there is a basic conflict between these two approaches to the physical world, in that the theories of relativity place a speed limit on the transfer of information, energy and matter, whereas the quantum theory strongly suggests that this speed limit can be transgressed under certain circumstances. The current state of play in this respect is well stated by John Bell, in the following extracts taken from an introductory lecture he gave at a Naples/Amalfi meeting on 7 May 1984, entitled 'Speakable and Unspeakable in Quantum Mechanics'. He started his lecture with a quotation from Arthur Koestler's *The Sleepwalkers*:

... the history of cosmic theories may without exaggeration be called a history of collective obsessions and controlled schizophrenias; and the manner in which some of the most important discoveries were arrived at reminds one of a sleepwalker's performance ...

'For many decades now our fundamental theories have rested on the two great pillars to which this meeting is dedicated; quantum theory and relativity,' Bell said and, after a very brief summary of some recent progress, he continued:

In the manner in which this progress is made, will we see again any elements of Koestler's picture? Certainly we will see nothing like the obsessive commitment of the old heroes to their hypotheses. Our theorists take up and put down hypotheses with light hearts, playfully. There is no religious intensity in it. And certainly no fear of becoming involved in litigation with the religious authorities. As for technical mistakes, our theorists do not make them. And they see at once what is important and what is detail. So it is another feature of contemporary progress which reminds me of the title of Koestler's book. This progress is made in spite of the fundamental obscurity in quantum mechanics. Our theorists stride through that obscurity unimpeded ... sleepwalking?

The progress so made is immensely impressive. If it is made by sleepwalkers, is it wise to shout 'wake up'? I am not sure that it is. So I speak now in a very low voice.

He ended his talk with the following words:

For me then this is the real problem with quantum theory: the apparently essential conflict between any sharp formulation and fundamental relativity. This is to say, we have an apparent incompatibility, at the deepest level, between the two fundamental pillars of contemporary theory ... and of our meeting. I am glad therefore that in some sessions we will stand back from the impressive technical details of current progress to review this strange situation. It may be that a real synthesis of quantum and relativity theories requires not just technical developments but radical conceptual renewal.

5 | The Fabric of Matter

To see a World in a Grain of Sand
 And heaven in a Wild Flower,
Hold Infinity in the palm of your hand,
 And Eternity in an hour.

William Blake, 'Auguries of Innocence'

In the world-line web of quantum reality, which is introduced in this chapter, it is proposed that all charged particles leave permanent trails in space-time, in the form of a 'polarized' world line. Thus as particles move through space-time, interacting with each other in the process, they are weaving a world-line web. The 'polarized' points of space on the web become sequenced by the passage of particles through space-time, and they will remain sequenced in this way. Ordinary space is made up of the spaces between the web. Different laws apply to the world-line web and ordinary space. It is proposed that the vibrations of the threads of the world-line web are the pilot waves first proposed by Louis de Broglie. It is further proposed that all the so-called elementary particles are localized 'windings' of these polarized world lines, and their masses and other properties arise from the qualities of these world lines and the nature of the 'windings'. Before discussing the theory in more detail, we will briefly discuss some other current approaches to the structure of matter. In many cases we will use the words of the supporters of alternative theories, just to give a flavour of the rigour of the ongoing debate.

The Structure of Matter

The Quark Theory of Matter

At one stage in the history of science, scientists believed that the chemical elements consisted of indivisible particles called atoms. In Chapter 2 we saw that the work of Rutherford and Bohr showed us

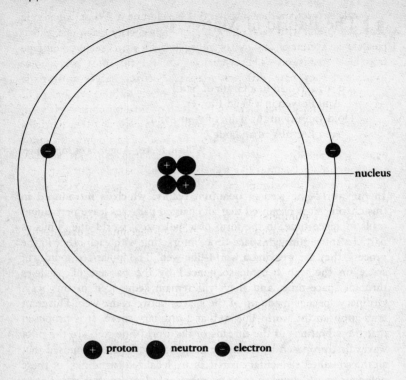

+ proton ● neutron — electron

5.1 *A schematic view of the helium atom showing the electrons orbiting the central nucleus.*

that this was not the case. They conceived a model of the atom in which most of the mass was concentrated in the nucleus, which had a positive electric charge, and this nucleus was orbited by less massive electrons; in some respects, this model resembled the way the planets orbited the Sun (see Fig. 5.1). It was later shown that the nucleus itself was made up of two types of particle, called protons and neutrons. The masses of these two types of particle were very similar, but they were about two thousand times more massive than the electron. The charge on the proton was equal in magnitude, but opposite in sign to the charge on the electron. In a neutral atom the number of protons in the nucleus is equal to the number of electrons orbiting the nucleus.

Quarks are yet another stage in this development. When subatomic particles collide with each other in vast high-energy machines, called particle accelerators, a host of other particles are seen to emerge from such collisions. These particles are for the most part short-lived, and they have different masses, electric charges and spins. Charge and spin seemed to come only in whole numbers or halves of whole numbers, so they came to be called quantum numbers. It soon emerged that more quantities are required to classify these particles on the basis of their behaviour. Most of these other quantities cannot be associated with physical concepts, like charge and spin, so they are given abstract names like hypercharge and isospin, but they also generally come in integers and half-integers, so they are also called quantum numbers.

Using these numbers, and arranging the particles according to the values of their quantum numbers, it soon becomes apparent that they fall into very neat patterns. Scientists have been surprised by these patterns, but they were even more surprised to find that these patterns can be represented in a very simple way if one assumes that all the members of a particular class of particle – called hadrons – are made up of a small number of elementary entities. These entities, quarks, were postulated by M. Gell-Mann and G. Zweig in 1963. Independently, these two scientists succeeded in accounting for all the regularities by assigning appropriate quantum numbers to three quarks and their antiquarks. Putting these quarks together in various combinations they were also able to form two other classes of particles – called baryons and mesons – whose quantum numbers are simply obtained by adding those of their constituent quarks. Baryons, in this scheme, consist of three quarks, their corresponding antiparticles of the corresponding antiquarks, and mesons of a quark plus an anti-quark.

Although the quark model continues to be very successful in accounting for the regularities found in the particle world, it is no longer used in its original simple form, and particle physicists have had to introduce additional quarks to account for the large variety of hadron patterns. The simple quark model leads to severe difficulties, in spite of its efficiency and simplicity, if the quarks are considered to be the physical constituents of hadrons. The forces that hold particles together are supposed to be carried by other particles which are exchanged between the interacting particles. This means that these exchanged particles must also be present inside hadrons. If this were indeed the case, then they too would contribute to the properties of the hadrons and this would destroy the simple additive scheme of the quark model. These are some of the problems which have led some physicists to propose an alternative approach to high-energy physics.

Superstrings

In recent years a new theory of the fundamental particles has arisen. This approach to the elementary particles is founded largely in the work of John Schwarz and Michael Green. They propose that all particles are made up of mathematical entities called strings. One of the reasons for developing this theory was the fact that the quarks that made hadrons had to be held together in some way, and one could see the strings as a way of describing this interaction. Since the interacting force was so great, the strings had to be extremely strong. It was thus possible to picture the quark, not as a separate entity in its own right, but rather as a particular state of vibration of the string. Since such strings could vibrate as well as rotate it was then possible to see other particles as different modes of vibration and rotation of the basic strings. Superstring theory has problems of its own. It soon became apparent that theories based on the string concept would have to have more than the four dimensions of space-time. The first theories made use of twenty-six dimensions, but the newer superstring theory has ten dimensions. In answer to the question of why we are only aware of the three dimensions of space and one of time, physicists say that the other dimensions are compactified within the small region of space which we identify as an elementary particle.

In the new superstring theory of physics, the physicists are literally trying to tie all the loose ends of physics together to produce a theory of everything, from the basic forces of physics to the so-called elementary particles. This approach has divided the physics community.

Richard Feynman had this to say regarding superstring theory:

No, I don't know whether you'd call it a style of research, it's a question of verifying your ideas against experiment and whether the theory is precise enough. It is precise mathematically, but the mathematics is far too difficult for the individuals who are doing it, and they don't draw their conclusions with any rigour. So they just guess.

Professor Steven Weinberg, another Nobel prizewinner in physics, has a different point of view:

The final theory is going to be what it is because it's mathematically consistent. Then the physical interpretation will come only when you solve the theory and see what it predicts for physics at accessible energies. This is physics in a realm which is not directly accessible to experiment, and the guiding principle can't be physical intuition because we don't have any intuition for dealing with that scale. The theory has to be conditioned by mathematical consistency. We hope this will lead to a theory with solutions that look like the real world at accessible energies. I'm afraid that the usual physical insight based on experience with experiments in physics isn't a great deal of help here.

S Matrix and Bootstrap

Over the last few decades another approach to elementary particles has been investigated. This is an approach based on a mathematical device called the S matrix. Fritjof Capra explains the central feature of this approach in the following words:

The important new concept in S-matrix theory is the shift of emphasis from objects to events; its basic concern is not with the particles, but with their reactions.

Werner Heisenberg had previously made a similar point:

. . . one has divided the world not into different groups of objects but into different groups of connections . . . What can be distinguished is the kind of connection which is primarily important in a certain phenomenon . . . The world thus appears as a complicated tissue of events, in which connections of different kinds alternate or overlap or combine and thereby determine the texture of the whole.

The idea of the 'bootstrap' has also arisen in the context of this theory. It is described by Capra in the following words:

There is, however, a radically different school of thought in particle physics which starts from the idea that nature cannot be reduced to fundamental entities, such as elementary particles or fundamental fields. It has to be understood entirely through its self-consistency, with its components being consistent both with one another and with themselves. This idea has arisen in the context of S-matrix theory and is known as the 'bootstrap' hypothesis. Its originator is Geoffrey Chew, who . . . has used it (in collaboration with other physicists) to construct a specific theory of particles formulated in S-matrix language.

Capra says:

The new approach culminated in the concept of the ordered S matrix which made it possible to derive results characteristic of quark models without any need to postulate the existence of physical quarks. These results have generated great enthusiasm among S-matrix theorists, many of whom now believe that we shall be able, in the not-too-distant future, to go beyond the quark model; to do, as it were, quark physics without quarks.

As things stand in the scientific community at the moment, there are three contenders for a theory concerning the basic particles of matter and their interactions. The first is the quark theory, which is not only the most popular, but is also the one that is the most fully developed. The second contender is superstring theory, which has a growing number of supporters, but so far it is not as highly developed as the quark theory, since it is not yet possible to calculate some of the most important properties of the elementary particles. The third theory is S-matrix theory coupled with the bootstrap hypothesis. This has very few supporters and it is also unable, as yet, to rival the predictions obtained from the quark theory. I want to propose a fourth alternative, which offers the possibility of understanding the interactions between the so-called basic particles of matter, and the apparent conflict between relativity and quantum theory; it also opens the door to an understanding of phenomena which we currently classify as paranormal.

The Plasma Space Theory of Matter

The Structure of the Elementary Particles

An ordinary gas consists of neutral atoms in which the number of protons in the nucleus is exactly balanced by the number of electrons orbiting the nucleus. The movements of such atoms are not influenced by magnetic fields. A plasma is a very hot gas, in which the atoms are moving so fast that some of their electrons have been stripped away by collisions with other atoms. Such atoms thus have electrical charges and they are called ions. These ions and the free electrons do interact with magnetic fields, in that they will spiral around the 'lines of force' used to represent the direction of the magnetic field. They will thus behave as if they are 'threaded' to the lines of force in a way not dissimilar to the way that beads are threaded to the string of a necklace. If the ions and the electrons are moved then the lines of force will also move, and if the lines of force are moved so will the ions and the electrons. I am proposing that there are two different types of space – ordinary space and plasma space. The points of ordinary space are rather like neutral atoms in that they are not 'threaded' by 'lines of force'. The points in plasma space are 'threaded' by 'electric lines of force'.

The plasma space theory of matter proposes an analogy between the ions of a material plasma and the points of plasma space, and between the magnetic lines of force that thread the plasma and the electric lines of force that thread their way through plasma space. It further proposes that just as there are no ends to magnetic lines of force there are no ends to electric lines of force. The electric lines of force are completely frozen into plasma space from the beginning of time and the 'fluid' of plasma space within the so-called elementary particles is incompressible. The basic particle of matter in this theory is the neutron. The 'core' of the neutron is a force-free 'ball of yarn' configuration of electric lines of force, and this gives the neutron its mass. This means that the neutron has energy by virtue of the electric energy compactified within it. When the neutron decays it is the outer unstable cloak of lines of force that rearranges itself to give the proton–electron configuration and a neutrino. There are then three stable particles: the proton, electron and neutrino. The core of

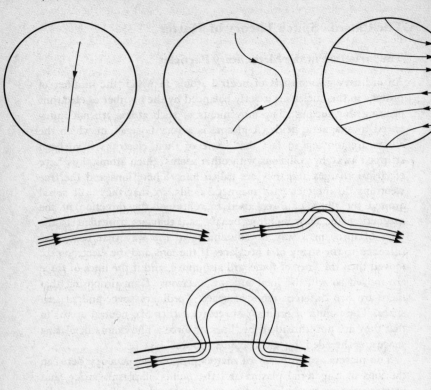

5.2 (*a*) *A magnetic line of force beneath the Sun's surface will be wound up because the gases near the solar equator rotate faster than those near the poles.*

(*b*) *The resulting tube of force, just beneath the surface, will become buoyant; it will then buckle and rise above the surface to form a loop prominence, and the points at which it crosses the solar surface will become a pair of sunspots.*

each of these particles is a force-free 'ball of yarn' configuration of electric lines of force embedded in the plasma space confined within these particles. The neutrino has no charge so it is just a compacted 'ball of yarn' of electrified plasma space.

The decay of the neutron resembles, to some extent, the formation of a solar prominence and a sunspot pair (see Fig. 5.2). When it decays, the outer shell of the neutron, because it is unstable, will rearrange itself in such a way that the lines of force will splay outwards from the neutron to form a proton, will wrap themselves around the core of the new electron, which has been ejected, and will then twist back to the proton in an extremely thin bundle of electrified plasma space. Because of the way the lines of force are twisted in this bundle, it behaves as if it were encased in an insulating tube of space (see Fig. 5.3). Such a configuration is called a force-free field, because it does not exert a direct physical force outside the bundle. This means that although the fibre bundle of electrified plasma space can push particles about, in much the same way that a magnetic field can, via ions, push atoms about, it does not interact with these particles directly, via electric forces. In the process a 'ball of yarn' configuration of electrified plasma space is produced, of extremely small size and hence very little mass – this is the neutrino. The electrified plasma space within the cores of the proton, electron and neutrino is incompressible, but the electrified plasma space in the tube bundle taking lines of force back from the electron to the proton is capable of being stretched to astronomical distances. The 'ball of yarn' configurations within the electron and proton (and within a neutron in a stable nucleus) are all spinning on their own axes, and thus they will behave like little magnets. It is this behaviour that gives rise to the measurable 'magnetic moments' of these particles. The difference between these particles and their corresponding antiparticles lies in the difference in direction between the spinning of these 'balls of yarn' and the direction in which the lines of force are wound on each 'yarn'. For antiparticles it is in the opposite direction to what it is for particles.

Plasma Space Theory and the Evolution of the Universe

Before the 'Big Bang' all the electrified plasma space was confined to a very small volume. It was the electric pressure in this volume that led to the expansion of the universe. Initially, after a small expansion, the electric plasma space fragmented into a large number of neutrons, which could exist because they were still in close proximity to each other. It is just as if in 'the global village' of the early universe a 'stable marriage' could exist between an electron and proton and the neutrino was the 'wedding ring' of the marriage. Originally there was just a tangled loop of electrified plasma space, so a large number of reconnections had to take place to produce the neutrons. This

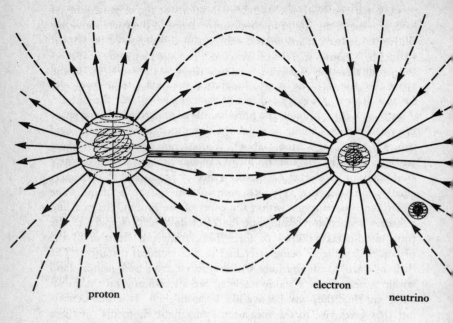

proton

electron

neutrino

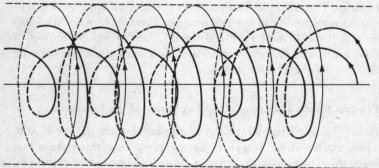

5.3 (a) *The plasma space configuration of a proton, electron and neutrino.*

(b) *The force-free plasma space configuration linking the electron back to the proton.*

process, together with the unstable vibrations of the original tangled loop, produced the high radiation temperature of the early universe. With the further expansion and subsequent dispersion of the global village the 'neutron marriages' dissolved, and the neutrinos produced as a result were the discarded 'wedding rings'. At a later stage in the history of the universe 'neutron marriages' could exist in the much smaller villages of stable nuclei.

The eventual recycling of matter in the early universe, in galaxies, in stars, on the Earth and in living matter has meant that the electrons have become separated from the protons to which they were once married. A graphic description of the type of recycling that takes place in stars is to be found in Sir Arthur Eddington's *The Internal Constitution of the Stars*:

The inside of a star is a hurly-burly of atoms, electrons and ether waves. We have to call to aid the most recent discoveries of atomic physics to follow the intricacies of the dance ... Try to picture the tumult! Dishevelled atoms tear along at fifty miles a second with only a few tatters left of their elaborate cloaks of electrons torn from them in the scrimmage. The lost electrons are speeding a hundred times faster to find new resting-places. Look out! There is nearly a collision as an electron approaches an atomic nucleus; but putting on speed it sweeps round it in a sharp curve. A thousand narrow shaves happen to the electron in 10^{-10} of a second; sometimes there is a side-slip at the curve, but the electron still goes on with increased or decreased energy. Then comes a worse slip than usual; the electron is fairly caught and attached to the atom, and its career of freedom is at an end. But only for an instant. Barely has the atom arranged the new scalp on its girdle when a quantum of ether waves runs into it. With a great explosion the electron is off again for further adventures. Elsewhere two of the atoms are meeting full tilt and rebounding, with further disaster to their scanty remains of vesture.

Eddington's description is a classic piece of science writing. Even in his day the concept of the ether had already been replaced by that of the electromagnetic field. He was using the concept as a literary device. Thus where he uses the term 'ether waves' it should be understood that he is referring to electromagnetic waves.

The electric lines of force go from the proton to the electron in normal space, but they go from the electron back to the proton in the opposite direction in plasma space. This means that as an electron or proton describes its world line in space-time, this world line has a physical reality in the form of a fibre bundle of electrified plasma space. The recycling and evolution of matter means that the whole of space is criss-crossed by an interconnecting and interwoven web of such world lines, rather like a disordered spider's web.

The Laws of Normal Space and Plasma Space

The normal space we investigate with scientific equipment and known to us through our senses is the space between the threads of the web. The measured speed of light is the limiting speed in normal space. Interactions between particles whose world lines have crossed in the past can take place faster than the speed of light. The particles retain 'memories' of their past interactions. However, it is only the recent 'memories' that are retained unambiguously. The older 'memories' are 'degraded' by the number of interactions that lie between them and the present. The separate forms of matter are nothing more than colonies within the web. As the universe expands, so the lines of electric force of the web stretch and the size of the spaces between the web increases. The large-scale colonies of matter have mass as a result of the localized energy embedded within them, and as they move through the web of world lines they merely brush them aside, or trail them behind, without interacting with them in any other way. Large masses thus do not respond to the continuous and eternal vibrations of the world-line web, and so they obey the laws of Newtonian physics. Subatomic particles do feel the vibrations of the web, and as a result they obey a rather different set of laws. These are the laws of quantum mechanics.

Professor David Bohm attributed quantum mechanical effects to the fluctuations of a special field which he called the psi-field: 'The fluctuations of the psi-field can be regarded as coming from a deeper sub-quantum level, in much the same way that fluctuations in the Brownian motion of a microscopic liquid droplet come from a deeper atomic level.' (Brownian motion is the incessant movement of tiny particles of dirt or dust suspended in a liquid. The movement of these dust particles, which is random in direction, can be seen in a drop of liquid when viewed under a microscope. It arises from the bombarding of the particles of dust, which are much larger than atoms, by the atoms. The phenomenon was first discovered by Robert

Brown in 1827, and it was treated theoretically by Albert Einstein in the first decade of our own century.)

The plasma space theory of matter says that the fluctuations of the psi-field are due to the world-line web.

'Polynesian Navigators' of the Quantum World

The last few pages may have been difficult to follow for some people. Here is an analogy which should help to clarify some consequences of the theory I am proposing.

The seamen of Polynesia navigate their way around the Polynesian islands using a variety of navigational aids. One of their methods makes use of the pattern of ocean swells that exist around the islands. The waves coming from the open ocean will be reflected from the beaches of the mainland, but when there is an island off the mainland, the incoming waves and the reflected waves will interact with each other to give rise to an interference pattern around the island. If there are a number of islands then there will be an even more complex interference pattern around them. The young navigators of the islands are taught how to use the bobbing up and down of their boats to detect the amplitudes and directions of the various waves, and hence to deduce from this, and a map of the interference pattern, their approximate position with respect to the islands. This is a rather simple and natural version of the more modern navigational systems that make use of radio-wave interference patterns generated by radio transmitters on land which we discussed in Chapter 3. I am proposing that subatomic particles navigate using a similar method.

In an ordinary plasma, consisting of neutral atoms (or molecules) and ions, there are two types of wave that can propagate through it. There are the ordinary sound waves which propagate in all directions, and which involve atoms and ions, and then there are Alfvén waves. Michael Faraday believed that magnetic-field lines behave as if they have tension along their lengths; the concept was given mathematical substance by the work of Hannes Alfvén. This means that if one plucks a field line it will vibrate, rather like the plucked string of a violin. It is this vibration that we call an Alfvén wave, and it propagates along the field line with the Alfvén speed. The speed of sound is related to the pressure and density of the plasma, but the Alfvén speed is related to the strength of the magnetic field and its density. The two speeds can be very different. In a strong magnetic field the Alfvén speed can be much higher than the speed of sound. It is also confined to where there is a magnetic field. I am proposing that ordinary electromagnetic waves propagate through ordinary space at the speed of light, but 'Alfvén space' waves can propagate along the electrified world lines of the world-line web which permeates the cosmos. The speed of Alfvén space waves can exceed the speed of light, and thus these waves are the pilot waves, first proposed by Prince Louis de Broglie (see p. 56), which inform subatomic particles where to go.

Plasma Space and the Elementary Particles

Geophysicists working on the theory of how the Earth's magnetic field may be generated by the motions of the fluid parts of its interior described the structure of the internal field, and the flow lines of the fluid's motion, in terms of a special type of mathematical function called spherical harmonics. This type of mathematical function can also be used to describe the shape of a sphere that has been distorted in any way. Simple shapes can be represented by spherical harmonics which have just one or two maxima and minima associated with them, and these are called low-order harmonics. More complex shapes use harmonics with several maxima and minima – these are called high-order harmonics (see Fig. 5.4). These harmonics were first introduced into mathematics by the French mathematician Laplace, who built on the work of another French mathematician, Legendre. Both men were trying to find a way of working out the gravitational field of planets that were not exactly spherical. These functions are now very extensively used in many applications of mathematics. They are used to describe the shapes of the planets and the structure of their gravitational and magnetic fields. On a very much larger scale, while doing research for my MSc and PhD, I pioneered the use of spherical harmonics to determine the structure and symmetry properties of the vast magnetic field that threads its way through the whole Milky Way galaxy. On a much smaller scale they are used to describe the structure of the atom in terms of quantum-mechanical wave functions (see Fig. 5.5). The use of these harmonics in atomic structure has yielded many results that have

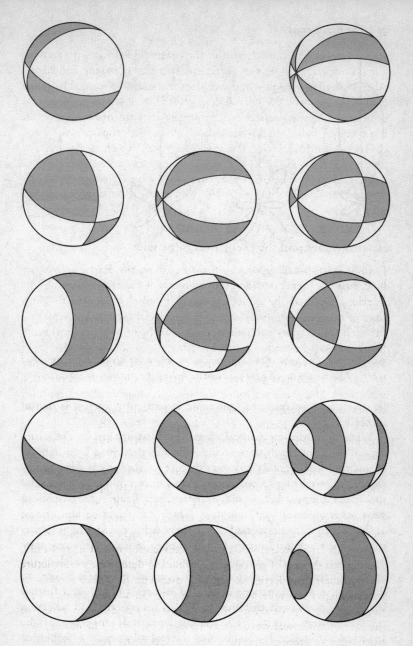

5.4 *A pictorial representation of some of the spherical harmonics. The dark regions on the spheres are concave and the grey regions are convex.*

5.5 *The wave functions of the hydrogen atom, which are derived from the use of spherical harmonics to solve the equation describing the structure of the atom.*

far-reaching consequences. One topic of particular interest is that of forbidden lines.

When quantum-mechanical ideas were first applied to the structure of the atom, each state of the atom was described by a number of quantum numbers. It was soon discovered that atoms were generally not allowed to go from certain states to certain other states, and the spectral lines that would have resulted from such transitions were never observed in a laboratory. These transitions became known as 'forbidden transitions', and this concept led to the idea of 'selection rules' which quantum numbers had to obey in going from one state to another. With the development of Schrödinger's model of the atom, it became clear that spherical harmonics were necessary to describe the wave functions associated with this model, and further investigations showed that the 'forbidden transitions' and 'selection rules' followed directly from the mathematical properties of the spherical harmonics. It also clarified the real meaning of a 'forbidden transition'. It showed they were linked to states that had extremely long 'lifetimes' and that in the high densities of terrestrial laboratories atoms would undergo collisions with other atoms before they were 'allowed' to 'decay' from these states, and as a result they would be excited into a different state, with a shorter lifetime, from which they could decay more rapidly. However, in the extremely low densities and large volumes that one quite often encountered in gas clouds between the stars it was possible to observe these 'forbidden transitions'.

In extending the theory of plasma space to discussing elementary particles, the internal structure of the electric field within a proton, neutron or neutrino is also described in terms of these spherical harmonics. Because protons and neutrons can both exist in the nuclei of atoms, they are given the collective name of nucleons. When nucleons were bombarded with electrons it seemed as if they had some internal structure, and this structure was attributed to the quarks we have already discussed. According to the plasma space theory of the elementary particles, the collision between an electron and a nucleon will excite the nucleon into states that can be described by higher-order harmonics, and these higher states will cause the electron to be deflected, or scattered, in a way that will give the impression that the nucleon has internal structure. Many different collisions between a large variety of particles have revealed a plethora of so-called elementary particles, most of which are extremely short-lived. These particles can be described by sets of quantum numbers, and these numbers follow particular patterns, enabling physicists studying high-energy particles to group the particles into families. The plasma space theory of matter would say that these short-lived particles are not particles at all. They are the result of collisions which excite the known stable particles into states described by high-order harmonics, which we will call multipole extensions of the original fields of these particles, and the subsequent fragmentation of such a multipole will give rise to so-called short-lived particles which are not really elementary at all!

The work of Bullard and Gellman, on how internal motions of plasmas can convect magnetic fields to generate new magnetic configurations, showed that these fields also obey 'selection rules' and these, once again, arise from the mathematical properties of the spherical harmonics used to describe the field and the internal motions of the plasma. They also showed that these 'selection rules' gave rise to whole families of magnetic configurations which exhibited remarkable symmetry properties. The plasma space theory of elementary particles proposes that the quantum numbers associated with the discovered families of 'elementary particles', and the patterns that arise within these families, are the result of the mathematical properties of the spherical harmonics which are used to describe the internal fields of the stable particles as well as the relative motions of the fields. The rules that govern particle collisions, and the symmetry properties of the resulting families of particles, can once again be considered to rise from the mathematical properties of the spherical harmonics. The ancient concept of 'the music of the spheres' seems to manifest itself at a variety of levels in the physical universe, from the very large to the very small.

At the end of the last chapter of a recent version of the *Tao of Physics*, which Capra entitled 'The New Physics Revisited', he has this to say regarding Bohm's theory, which we discussed in Chapter 4, and Chew's theory (see p. 68):

At present, Bohm's theory is still at a tentative stage and, although he is developing a mathematical formalism involving matrices and topology, most of his statements are qualitative rather than quantitative. Nevertheless, there seems to be an intriguing kinship, even at this preliminary stage, between his theory of the implicate order and Chew's bootstrap theory. Both approaches are based on the same view of the world as a dynamic web of relations; both attribute a central role to the notion of order; both use matrices to represent change and transformation, and topology to classify categories of order. Finally, both approaches recognize that consciousness may be an essential aspect of the universe that will have to be included in a future theory of physical phenomena. Such a future theory may well arise from the merging of the theories of Bohm and Chew, which represent two of the most imaginative and philosophically profound approaches to physical reality.

It may well be that the approaches of Bohm and Chew, when worked out in abstract mathematical terms, will lead to a more refined view of reality. I myself do not think that Western science is quite ready, culturally, for such a profound philosophical change in its basic belief system. The theory I have proposed in this chapter is a more concrete model of physical reality, which can be seen as an intermediate rung in the never-ending ladder of our attempts to get closer to the 'heaven of ultimate cosmic reality'.

6 | Magnetic Memories

> As I proceeded with the study of Faraday, I perceived that his method of conceiving phenomena [of electromagnetism, in terms of lines of force] was also a mathematical one, though not exhibited in the conventional form of mathematical symbols. I also found that these methods were capable of being expressed in the ordinary mathematical forms, and thus compared with those of the professed mathematicians.
>
> James Clerk Maxwell, *A Treatise on Electricity and Magnetism* (1873)

One of the outstanding achievements of modern science has been to show that a great deal of the diversity and complexity of the universe, from the subatomic scale right up to the scale of the galaxies, can, in principle, be understood in terms of four fundamental forces. In this chapter I shall briefly outline the nature of these forces, the roles that three of them play in astronomy, and the eternal marriage between electricity and magnetism. I shall then go on to discuss the nature of magnetic memories, terrestrial, cosmic and technological.

The Forces of Physics

The four fundamental forces are: the strong nuclear force; the weak nuclear force; gravitation; and the electromagnetic force. The nuclear forces are very short in range and act only over distances comparable in size with the nucleus of the atom, which is very much smaller than the atom itself. Gravitation is the weakest of all the forces, but it acts between all bodies that have mass, and it is long range, acting over large distances which are comparable in size to the distances separating planets, stars and galaxies. The electromagnetic force has two sides to it. It is an expression of the very close link between electricity and magnetism. It acts at a great variety of levels, from the very small to the very large. Since it is the basis of the force that holds atoms, molecules and any large aggregates of matter (larger than molecules but smaller than planets) together, it is of great importance to all scientists and technologists. In other words the electromagnetic force plays an essential role in those parts of the universe that are encountered in the local environment and everyday life.

Nuclear Forces in Astronomy

We have already seen that the nuclei of atoms are made up of two different types of particles; one type is called the neutron and the other type is called the proton. The masses of proton and neutron are very nearly the same, but they are both almost two thousand times the mass of the electron. The proton has a positive electrical charge, the neutron has no charge and the electron has a negative electrical charge. It is the electrical attraction between the electrons and the protons which keeps the atom together. If we represent the size of the atom, to scale, by the size of a baseball stadium, then the nucleus is about the size of the baseball. This means that the atom is mostly empty space.

It is a well-known fact of electricity that like charges repel each other, while unlike attract each other. As we have already seen, it is the attraction between the electrons and the protons, which have opposite charges, that keeps the electrons bound in orbits about the central nucleus. Since the protons within a nucleus all have the same charge, they will want to repel each other, yet in all atoms, with the exception of hydrogen, protons exist in extremely close proximity with each other. This means that there must be a sort of 'superglue' which is strong enough to keep the protons and the neutrons together in the central nucleus. This is the strong nuclear force. Many particle physicists now believe that neutrons and protons are made up of yet smaller particles called quarks, and that the strong nuclear force is a remnant of a much more powerful force, called the colour force, acting on quarks inside the protons and neutrons.

The weak nuclear force operates when a neutron decays into a proton, emitting an electron and a neutrino. It thus plays a part in the radioactive decay of many nuclei. The most important role of nuclear forces in astronomy is in providing the source of energy in the deep interiors of stars. Here the temperatures are so high that the nuclei are moving very fast when they collide with each other, and so they are able to get close enough for the superglue to take effect before they repel each other. This means that nuclear reactions can take place within stars, in which the fusion of two nuclei can occur with the consequent release of enormous amounts of energy. This process is not only responsible for providing the stars with energy, it is also largely responsible for the manufacture of heavier elements from lighter ones. Because nuclear forces are short range and can only act when neutrons and protons are virtually in contact with each other, they cannot directly influence the area outside the reacting core of the star, but they can do so indirectly by means of particles (such as neutrinos) and electromagnetic radiation, which are produced as a result of nuclear reactions.

Gravitation and Astronomy

Gravitation is an interaction which occurs between every pair of particles in the universe. According to Newton's law of gravitation the force between any two particles is directly proportional to the product of their masses, and inversely proportional to the square of the distance between them. The one exception to this rule is the neutrino, which, as we have already mentioned, is a subatomic particle associated with some types of radioactive decay. Even the photon – the particle associated with electromagnetic radiation – is subject to gravitational interaction because it possesses energy, and hence, by Einstein's famous equation linking mass and energy, it also has mass. Newton's law implies that the force of attraction between two bodies gets weaker as the distance between them is increased. The weakening of the force by distance means that in most cases the gravitational influences of very distant objects can be ignored, even if they are massive. So, when we stand on Earth, its gravitational field is by far the strongest one we experience. However, in discussing the tides of the ocean we must consider the gravitational pull of the Moon and the Sun. Because the Moon is nearer to the Earth than the Sun is, its influence on the tides is greater than that of the Sun, although the Sun is of course far more massive than the Moon. On a larger scale the motions of the planets around the Sun and the orbits of satellites around their respective planets are completely controlled by gravitational forces.

Given that gravitation plays so large a part in the structure and dynamics of the universe, what is the role of magnetic fields? Let us look first at the nature of electromagnetic forces.

Magnets and Magnetic Fields

Most of us are familiar with the basic properties of magnets, either from recollections of school science lessons or through the use of magnets at home or at work. Probably the best-known property of a magnet is the ability to attract certain materials without any physical contact, and this attractive influence can penetrate certain other materials and substances. For instance, magnetic earrings are kept in place by a small magnet placed behind the ear, so the attractive force of the magnet is capable of penetrating the live tissue of the earlobe, without of course harming it in any way. The region of influence surrounding the magnet is called the magnetic field.

A simple way to show the existence and extent of this field is to sprinkle iron filings on a sheet of cardboard placed on top of an ordinary bar magnet. When the card is tapped lightly the iron filings will be arranged by the magnetic field into a clear pattern. This shows that the magnetic field acts along lines, and the iron filings will align themselves along these 'lines of force'. The lines seem to radiate from the ends of the bar magnet and join together half-way along the magnet. If a small compass is brought close to one end of the magnet, the compass needle will point directly away from it, whereas if brought close to the other end the needle will point directly towards the magnet (see Fig. 6.1). The two points near the ends of the magnet from which the lines radiate are called the poles of the magnet. The poles can be found by placing a small compass at several points around the end of the magnet, marking the directions in which the compass needle points at each position, and drawing lines through these directions. The point of intersection of the straight lines defines the pole at each end of the magnet (see Fig. 6.2).

The magnetic lines of force are intangible lines along which a compass needle will point or along which iron filings will align themselves if free to move under the influence of the magnet. Although these lines should not be thought of as real physical entities, they are nevertheless an extremely useful scientific concept. Michael Faraday, the great English physicist and chemist who lived from

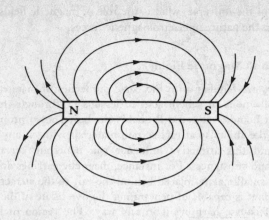

6.1 *Magnetic lines of force around a bar magnet.*

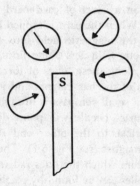

6.2 *Small search compasses pointing towards the pole of a bar magnet.*

1791 to 1867, was able to explain a great deal by giving these 'lines of force' real physical properties. He believed that the lines of force were something like elastic bands in that they tended to contract along their lengths. However, if there were a bundle of such lines all pointing in the same direction, then the lines would tend to repel each other at right angles to the direction in which they were pointing. In other words there is a tension along their lengths and a pressure at right angles to their lengths. The properties of magnets can be explained in terms of the interactions between these lines of force.

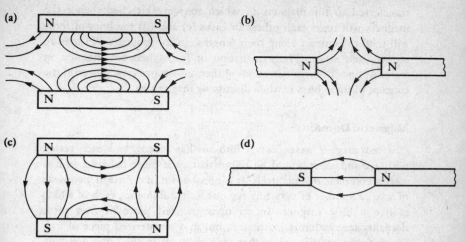

6.3 (*a*) *Lines of force around two bar magnets with like poles opposite each other.*

(*b*) *Lines of force around the facing like poles of two bar magnets.*

(*c*) *Lines of force around two bar magnets with unlike poles opposite each other.*

(*d*) *Lines of force around the unlike poles of two bar magnets.*

Suppose two bar magnets were marked with red paint at the ends to which a small compass needle points directly. If the two red-painted ends of the magnets are brought close to each other they will repel each other. However, if the painted end of one magnet is brought close to the unpainted end of the other magnet, they will attract each other. This shows that unlike poles attract each other and like poles repel each other. It is also possible to investigate the magnetic field surrounding these magnets when they are placed in different positions with respect to each other (Fig. 6.3). The magnets are stuck to a table top with sticky tape, and a sheet of card placed over them. Iron filings are sprinkled on to the card, which is then gently tapped. The configurations taken up by the iron filings will be as shown in Fig. 6.3. The directions in which the lines of force are pointing can be found using a small compass. In Figs. 6.3(a) and (b) the lines of force between the two magnets are pointing in the same direction, so the magnetic pressure between the lines will be transferred to the magnets to which they are attached: hence the magnets will repel each other. In cases (c) and (d) the lines of force will tend to contract along their lengths, so the magnets will tend to attract each other. The explanation of forces between magnets in terms of lines of force surrounding them illustrates how powerful the concept of these lines is when discussing magnetism.

Magnetic Domains

If a bar magnet were broken into smaller pieces, and each tested with a compass, it would be found that each piece behaved as if it were a complete magnet itself. It is now known that a magnet consists of a large number of very tiny regions, called domains, each of which is like a little magnet. In an unmagnetized piece of iron these domains are randomly orientated, but in a magnetized piece of iron the domains are aligned so that they all point in the same direction (see Fig. 6.4). This alignment can be achieved by stroking an unmagnetized piece of iron with a magnet (see Fig. 6.4(b)). If a magnet is heated above a certain temperature, which is known as the Curie point, it will cease to exhibit magnetic properties, and can only be re-magnetized once it has cooled below the Curie point. This can be explained in terms of the domain theory of magnetism. As the magnet is heated up the domains tend to move about more violently, and the violence of the movements will increase with temperature. Eventually a temperature will be reached where the domains move about so violently that they no longer sustain their original alignment, and the magnetism of the object is lost. If this unmagnetized iron is then allowed to cool in a magnetic field, for example the Earth's field, then at least some of the domains will become aligned in the field, and the iron will become slightly magnetized in the direction of the external field. The number of domains that will become aligned in the external field will depend on the strength of the field, hence the strength of the resulting magnet will be a measure of the strength of the field in which it cooled below the Curie temperature. This fact has been very useful in investigating the history of the Earth's field, and the application of this technique to the history of the Earth's field will be discussed later in the chapter.

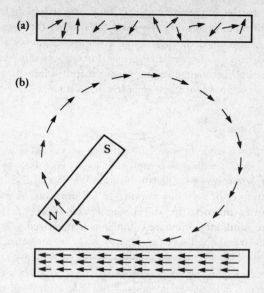

6.4 (*a*) *Unaligned domains in a soft iron bar.*

  (*b*) *Aligning the domains by stroking with a bar magnet.*

Electricity and Magnetism

Magnetic lines of force, or magnetic fields, can be generated by electric current, and electric current is itself the flow of electric charge. If an electric current passes through a coil of wire this will give rise to a magnetic field surrounding the coil. If this field is investigated using a small compass it will be noticed that it appears very similar to the magnetic field of a bar magnet (see Fig. 6.5). The lines of force form complete loops which thread their way through the interior of the coil. According to the modern theory of magnetic materials it is believed that the field lines of bar magnets also thread their way through the interiors of these magnets and that the field itself is generated by electric currents within the atoms of the iron from which the magnet is made.

A straight wire carrying an electric current produces a magnetic field in which the field lines take the form of concentric circles centred on the wire (see Fig. 6.6). Two parallel wires each carrying a

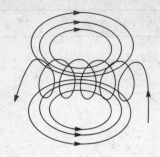

6.5 *Lines of force around a coil of wire.*

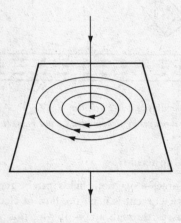

6.6 *Magnetic field around a straight conductor.*

current in the same direction will be attracted to each other. This attraction can also be explained in terms of the lines of force of their combined fields. The circular lines of each individual field will cancel in the region between the wires because they are in opposite directions. There will then be a reconnection of the lines forming the rest of the circles and the lines in the resulting loop will tend to contract along their lengths, giving rise to an attraction between the wires (Fig. 6.7).

Faraday also made the discovery that moving magnetic fields can produce electric currents. If a coil of wire is connected to a device

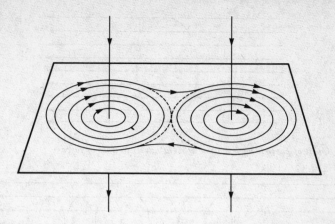

6.7 *Reconnections of lines of force around two straight conductors.*

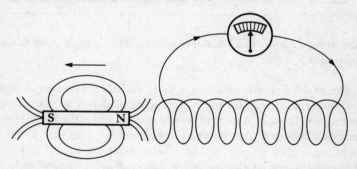

6.8 *Generating electric current by moving a magnet with respect to a coil of wire.*

for measuring electric current, called an ammeter, and a magnet is moved in and out of the coil, the ammeter registers a fluctuating current (see Fig. 6.8). In this experiment it does not really matter if the magnet is moved or the coil is moved – in either case an electric current is generated. This principle is the basis of the electric generator. All these experiments show how electricity and magnetism are intimately linked together.

A charged particle moving in a magnetic field experiences a force which is at right angles to the direction of its motion, and at right

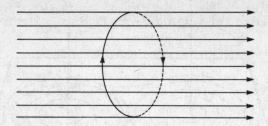

6.9 *Orbit of particle with motion at right angles to lines of force.*

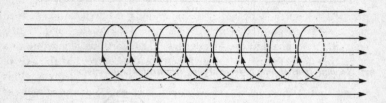

6.10 *Orbit of particle with direction of motion making an angle of less than 90 degrees with field lines.*

angles to the magnetic field (Fig. 6.9). If the field is extensive enough and uniform in strength, and the particle's motion is at right angles to the field lines, then its path will be a circle about the lines. If the particle's motion makes an angle with the field lines that is not a right angle, then its path will be a helix about the lines (Fig. 6.10). The principle of an electron being deflected by a magnetic field is used extensively in modern electrical equipment, for example in the scanning mechanism of a television set, or in an electron microscope.

A wire carrying an electric current consists of charges in motion within the wire, so these charges will experience a mechanical force if the wire is placed in a magnetic field. In particular, a small coil placed in a magnetic field has a field of its own, which is very similar to that of a bar magnet, so when a current is passed through it, it will tend to orientate itself with the plane of the coil at right angles to the external field. This principle is used in electrical measuring equipment and forms the basis of all electric motors.

The Nature of Magnetic Memories

The History of the Earth's Magnetic Field

Most of us have at some time made use of a magnetic compass to find direction. For hundreds of years sailors have used the compass to find their way across the sea. In this section we will look at how the Earth's magnetic field has changed with time, and the methods that have been used to investigate these changes. Before doing so it is necessary to define some terms associated with this magnetic field. The compass needle does not point to true north, but to magnetic north. True north is located at the north pole of Earth, and is defined as the northern point at which the Earth's axis cuts the surface. It is convenient to imagine the magnetic field of Earth as being due to a large bar magnet situated somewhere near the centre, but the axis of this magnet is inclined to the rotation axis by 11.5 degrees. This means that at most places the needle of a magnetic compass will not point to true north. The angle between true north and magnetic north at any place on the surface of Earth is called the magnetic declination of that location.

As the ordinary compass needle is only able to move freely in a plane parallel to the Earth's surface it cannot give us all the information we need to plot the magnetic lines of force of the Earth. In order to get more information we also need a magnetic needle that is able to move freely in a vertical plane. Such a device is called a dip circle. The angle between the horizontal and the needle of the dip circle, when the plane of its motion is parallel to the direction of the magnetic field at that point, is called the angle of dip or inclination.

There are three methods used to investigate the history of the Earth's field. Actual measurements of the strength, dip and declination covering a long period of time are the most direct methods of investigating long period changes. This is limited to the period for which accurate observations have been recorded, and systematic observations which can be used for this purpose only started in 1635. Accurate observations cover an even shorter period – from 1830 to the present day. These observations show that not only has there been a change in the strength of the field, but the positions of the geomagnetic poles have also changed.

The next method makes use of archaeological data. Many civilizations in various parts of the world had kilns which were baked to very high temperatures, and tiny magnetic fragments in the floors and walls of these kilns would be heated above the Curie temperature. This would mean, as explained earlier, that any magnetism present in the fragments would be destroyed. As the kilns cooled the tiny particles would be re-magnetized in the direction of the Earth's field as it was when the kiln was last fired. The number of fragments aligned by the field is related to the strength of the Earth's field at that time, so we can obtain information about the strength and direction of the field at various times by studying the magnetic particles in kilns from various ancient civilizations. This method is particularly useful for investigations of the field over the past few thousand years because in many cases the samples may be accurately dated using other archaeological methods. This method has shown that the strength of the magnetic field over this time scale has had a wavelike variation with a period of between 6,000 and 7,000 years, with a minimum at about 4000 BC and a maximum between 0 and AD 1000.

The third method is based on geological data and provides information on changes in the field covering a period of about five million years. This method is based on the fact that almost all rock contains small quantities of iron compounds and when a rock is formed it becomes magnetized in the direction of the Earth's field as it is at the time of formation. Once again, the strength of the magnetism is related to the strength of the field at that particular time. The age of the rock can be found by geological methods. The measurements made using this method produced the surprising result that the direction of the Earth's field has reversed several times during the last four and a half million years.

Tape Recorders, Video Tapes and Computers

Many examples of modern technological equipment, from tape recorders to computers, make use of magnetic memories. It is easy to explain how such a memory works for an ordinary tape recorder. One type of microphone consists of a diaphragm to which a small magnet is attached. This magnet is surrounded by a coil of wire. When sound waves strike the diaphragm of the microphone, it is set vibrating, and since the magnet is attached to this, it will also vibrate. As it vibrates in the surrounding coil, in which it is free to move, a small fluctuating electric current will be set up in this coil, and this can be amplified. In a public-address system this current is passed through a coil in the loudspeaker, in which another magnet, attached to the diaphragm of the speaker, is allowed to vibrate freely. The fluctuating current will cause this diaphragm to vibrate in unison with that of the microphone. In a tape recorder the second coil is used to align tiny magnetic fragments in a moving plastic tape. This means that the vibrations, which are pressure variations in time, are recorded as variations in the degree of alignment along the length of the tape. Thus the solid, but flexible, tape has stored on it a memory of the pressure variations in time. These pressure variations are recorded in the appropriate sequence. The same basic idea is used in the video recorder. Most information, whether it be variations of sound or light, or sequences of numbers and letters, can be put into some sort of code, and these variations or sequences can be stored as sequenced alignments of magnetic particles on a tape, a disc and a cash card.

It is possible to store magnetic memories in a solid because the sequencing of the alignments of the magnetic particles can be 'frozen' into the solid and, provided the solid is not heated above its Curie temperature or 'demagnetized' by placing it in a very strong rapidly fluctuating magnetic field, these memories can be retained indefinitely, because the atoms or molecules of the solid do not move with respect to each other. It is not possible, under normal circumstances, to record information in liquids or gases, because the atoms or molecules move with respect to each other, and so they cannot retain any sequencing for any length of time. There is, however, another state of matter which can, under special circumstances, retain a sequencing of its particles. This fourth state of matter is called the plasma state, and it is quite distinct from the other three states, solids, liquids and gases.

Magnetic Fields and the Plasma State of Matter

A plasma is a gas that is so hot that most of the atoms have been stripped of some of their outer electrons. Such atoms are called ions, and naturally, since the number of electrons orbiting the nucleus is less than the charge on the nucleus, these ions will have a positive charge. This means that the plasma will consist of free negatively charged electrons and positively charged ions.

The interaction between magnetic fields and plasmas has been investigated in terrestrial laboratories. This research was initiated because scientists have been trying to generate energy on Earth, using the same processes by which the Sun generates energy in its interior. But for these processes to work it is necessary to contain gases that have temperatures of several millions of degrees Celsius. Since these temperatures are so high, any solid container would just melt, so a method had to be found to keep the gases away from the walls of the container. This can be done using coils of wire, through which large currents of electricity are passing, to create a magnetic 'bottle' within the container. The study of the interactions between such magnetic configurations and plasmas has given rise to a very active branch of physics called plasma physics. It is easy to understand some of the basic ideas of the subject.

We have already seen that a plasma consists of positively charged ions and free electrons. If part of the plasma were moved across the magnetic lines of force of an external field, the charged particles will spiral around these lines, and since particles moving in such spirals are rather like electrons moving in a coil of wire, they will generate their own field. This means that the magnetic field in the plasma is a combination of the external field and the internally generated field. The original field plus the new internal field will have field lines which look as if the original field lines have just been displaced by the same amount as the part of the plasma that was moved. Physicists describe this phenomenon by saying that the magnetic field lines are frozen into the plasma. Earlier in the chapter the field lines were described as being like elastic bands in that they have a tendency to contract along their lengths. Hence the field lines will oppose the motion of a small volume of gas across them, and any attempt at such motion would meet with resistance like pulling on a taut elastic band. The field lines pointing in the same direction will tend to repel each other, thus giving rise to a magnetic pressure at right angles to the direction of the lines. This will be in addition to the normal gas pressure within the plasma.

Atoms, Electrons and Ions

James Clerk Maxwell formulated the kinetic theory of gases. According to this theory the atoms or molecules of a gas are in constant motion, colliding with each other and with the walls of the container in which it is placed. This constant motion is completely random and so there is no order in the positions or motions of the particles. Any particle or body that is moving has energy as a result of its motion. This energy is called kinetic energy, and it is proportional to the mass of the particle (or body) multiplied by the square of its speed; that is, its speed multiplied by itself. At a given temperature the molecules of a gas will have a spread of speeds, and thus also a spread of kinetic energies. However, one can use the laws of probability to calculate the average kinetic energy of all these particles, and it turns out that this average kinetic energy is directly proportional to the temperature of the gas. As one increases the temperature, so the average kinetic energy of the particles will increase and their average speeds will also increase.

In most plasmas not all the atoms will be ionized, and so we will have a mixture of neutral atoms, positive ions and negative electrons. If there is a magnetic field threading its way through the plasma, the ions and electrons will spiral around the lines of force, and so we can imagine that they are attached to these lines in much the same way as beads, in a string of beads, are attached to the loop of string on to which they are threaded. If one moves the string the beads move, and if one moves the beads then the string will move. If one moves the lines of force then the electrons and ions will move as well, and vice versa. The neutral atoms are not directly 'attached' to the lines of force, but because of numerous collisions between atoms, ions and electrons, they will take up any motion imparted to the ions and electrons by moving the lines of force.

Cosmic Plasmas and Memories

A great deal of matter in the universe is in the form of plasma. Some astronomers have estimated that more than 90 per cent of the cosmos is in the form of plasma. The very high temperatures in our Sun and other stars means that most of the gases of which these bodies are composed will be ionized – stripped of their electrons – and hence they will behave as a plasma. The planets of the solar system move within the outward flowing solar wind, which is a plasma. All the planets are surrounded by an aura of plasma. The vast spaces that separate the stars of our galaxy and other galaxies are filled with a very tenuous material called the interstellar medium, and much of this is in the form of plasma. Some of the planets have liquid interiors which behave in some respects like a plasma. We have already seen that there is a close interaction between plasmas and magnetic fields, and we now know that vast magnetic fields thread their way through all the plasmas we encounter in the universe.

The study of extraterrestrial magnetic fields started this century. By the end of the last century it was well established that the Earth had a magnetic field, and many of its properties had been investigated, including the fact that certain variations of the field were connected with the sunspot cycle. It had also been suggested in the last century, on the basis of the shape of the Sun's corona (the extended plasma envelope of the Sun which can be seen beyond the edge of the Moon during a total solar eclipse) that the Sun might also have a magnetic field. However, this suggestion had to await the observations of G. Hale and his co-workers before it was confirmed in 1908. At first progress was slow. By 1947 the solar magnetic field had been studied in some detail and H. D. Babcock had also measured stellar magnetic fields. The presence of magnetic fields in interstellar space was inferred from the polarization of starlight, which was measured by J. Hall and W. Hiltner in 1949.

In the last forty years progress has been much more rapid. This has largely been as a result of three separate factors: the first is the development of the new astronomies of radio, X-rays, infra-red and ultraviolet; the second, the use of space probes to investigate planetary and interplanetary environments; the third, vast improvements in the design of instrumentation for optical telescopes. All these techniques have considerably increased our knowledge of magnetic fields in the universe. It is now clear that some planets, many stars and several galaxies have magnetic fields which play varying roles in their structure and evolution.

It is important to study cosmic magnetic fields if we are to understand the structure, evolution and origin of our universe; to understand the links between our terrestrial and extraterrestrial environments; and to learn more about the interactions between plasmas and magnetic fields. The last point has been put very well by Professor E. Parker: 'Over astronomical dimensions the magnetic field takes on qualitative characteristics that are unknown in the terrestrial laboratory. The cosmos becomes the laboratory, then, in which to discover and understand the magnetic field and to apprehend its consequences.'

7 | Astrology, Prediction and Chaos

Then to the rolling Heav'n itself I cried,
Asking, 'What Lamp had Destiny to guide
　　Her little Children stumbling in the Dark?'
And – 'A blind Understanding!' Heav'n replied.
　　　　　Edward Fitzgerald, *The Rubáiyát of Omar Khayyám*

In this chapter we will discuss a theory of astrology which I have developed over the last few years. This theory is described in great detail in my book *Astrology: The Evidence of Science*. However, in this chapter I want to sketch the salient features of this theory and some more recent developments that are relevant to astrological predictions, and the frequent failure of such predictions. The reason for introducing this subject into the present book is that it is relevant to the topic of precognition, which will be discussed in a later chapter.

The theory consists of three separate, but connected, parts. The first part is concerned with the role the planets play in the overall control of solar magnetic activity and the way they trigger the onset of violent magnetic storms on the Sun. The second part of the theory is concerned with how this solar activity is transmitted to the Earth via the solar wind, how the interaction between the solar wind and the magnetosphere of Earth excites magnetic vibrations that respond directly to the tidal tug, due to gravitation, of the planets, and how the tidal tug of the Moon also contributes to the vibrations of the Earth's magnetic field. The third part of the theory is concerned with how the foetus, in the womb, interacts with the magnetic vibrations of the Earth. We will start by considering the evidence linking solar activity, planetary alignments and the aurorae.

Aurorae, Solar Tides and Planetary Alignments

On 13 March 1989 I witnessed a display of the northern lights in the skies just outside Plymouth. Mike Willmott, a friend and colleague, took some spectacular photographs of this outstanding display from his observatory at Widegates in Cornwall, a few miles from Plymouth. It is unusual, though not unheard of, to see the northern lights this far south. Normally such events only occur at these intermediate latitudes when sunspot activity is nearing, or at, its maximum. The last time I received a report of a display in this area, much less spectacular than the 1989 aurora, was in late January 1979. What is interesting is the positions of the planets on both occasions; in both instances there were three or more planets lined up with the Sun. Most astrologers would be prepared to believe that such alignments give rise to unusual events. Most scientists would dismiss the association as 'sheer coincidence' or 'meaningless mumbo-jumbo'. My theory of astrology can explain these observed correlations in scientific terms.

The Northern and Southern Lights

The northern and southern lights are a graphic and very visual demonstration of the interaction between the solar wind – a stream of very energetic subatomic particles emitted by the Sun – and the magnetic field of our Earth. Another name for the northern lights, which have for centuries evoked awe and wonder in people living in high latitudes, is the aurora borealis. Descriptions of the southern lights, or aurora australis, were first reported by Captain Cook in 1773. The general name for this whole class of phenomena is aurora polaris; it has been known since 1722 that occurrences of such phenomena are associated with changes in the Earth's field.

The aurorae can best be described as moving curtains of light. Mostly they are greenish-blue, but red aurorae are also seen on some occasions. The extensive use of all-sky cameras aboard fast jet planes, and, more recently, satellite observations, has helped geophysicists to determine the region in which the maximum number of aurorae occur. This region is called the auroral oval. The auroral light is emitted by atoms and molecules of different gases in the upper atmosphere, which have been excited by collisions with particles dumped into the magnetic field by the solar wind. The interaction of the solar wind with the magnetic field of Earth distorts the field, and also distorts the auroral oval. This distortion accounts for the fact that the auroral oval migrates to higher latitudes on the part of the Earth facing the Sun and to lower latitudes on the side facing away from the Sun. With increasing solar activity the auroral oval becomes wider and its lower boundary moves noticeably closer to the equator. This activity is related, in the theory developed by myself, to the effects of the planets on the Sun.

The Tides

Most of us have, at some stage of our lives, sat on a beach and watched the tide come in and go out again. We are all aware of the now accepted fact that this movement of the waters of the world is due to the gravitational tug of the Moon on the oceans, assisted, to a lesser extent, by the Sun. Although these facts are no longer in dispute, there were times when people were unwilling to accept that bodies so far from the Earth could have so direct an influence on our terrestrial environment.

In Chaucer's time people did not make a clear distinction between astronomy and astrology, and because they did not understand the scientific reasons for the tidal influence they attributed it to astrological causes. In 'The Franklin's Tale', however, Chaucer dismisses astrology, and its use to predict the tides, as an abominable superstition. The suggestion that the Moon might influence the oceans was also dismissed as 'occult nonsense' by the great scientist and astronomer Galileo.

It was Isaac Newton who gave scientific status to tidal prediction with his three laws of motion and his law of gravitation. He was able to show mathematically that when the Sun and the Moon were in a straight line with the Earth, either on the same side (as at new moon), or on opposite sides (as at full moon), then the difference between high tide and low tide would be at its greatest, and we would have the spring tides. When the Sun and Moon were at right angles to each other as seen from Earth, as at first and last quarters, then the difference between high and low tides would be at its least, and we would have neap tides. The link between the relative positions of Sun and Moon in the sky and the variation of tidal height, known before Newton, and explained in scientific terms by him, agreed to some extent with what astrologers had been claiming, not only about these bodies, but about the planets as well.

Planetary Aspects

The words 'square', 'conjunction' and 'opposition' are used to de-scribe the angles between any two planets as seen from Earth. If two planets are in the same part of the sky, they are in conjunction; if in opposite parts of the sky, they are in opposition. Square occurs when they are at right angles to each other. Such angles are called aspects by astrologers, and the angles just described are regarded as powerful by them. Astrologers also claim that angles of 30 and 150 degrees between any two planets, the Sun or the Moon, are slight in their influence, 60 degrees is fairly strong and 120 degrees is powerful. Newton's work showed that the tidal effects of Sun and Moon on the oceans were strongest at conjunctions and oppositions of these bodies, very weak at squares, and fairly weak at all the other angles mentioned. His law of gravitation also showed that the tidal forces of bodies increased with the size of the body causing it, and decreased, very rapidly, with the distance of the body from the Earth. This meant that it could apparently give no backing to any of the claims of astrologers concerning the planets, because they were too far away. There the subject remained until about forty years ago, when a radio engineer called John Nelson claimed that he had found some evidence supporting the views of astrologers, at least as far as 'radio weather' was concerned. At the time, Nelson was working for the Radio Corporation of America. He was given the task of trying to find a way of forecasting the occurrence of severe increases in solar activity, since it was generally thought that such increases could disrupt radio communications. Nelson discovered that when Venus, Earth, Mars, Jupiter and Saturn were in opposition or conjunction with respect to the Sun, or when they formed squares as seen from the Sun, conditions were likely to be particularly bad for radio reception. Conditions tended to be good when the angles between these planets, as seen from the Sun, were 30, 60, 120 and 150 degrees. (His results differ from the claims made by astrologers, since they claim that 30 and 150 degrees are weak, 60 degrees is fairly strong and 120 degrees is powerful, and they are referring to these angles between the planets as seen from the Earth.)

Nelson's work was analysed and discussed by various other scien-tists who found that the work contained several errors. Despite the fact that most of Nelson's work has been discredited, it did give rise to some more substantial investigations into the links between planetary configurations and solar activity. In the 1960s, another scientist, Paul Jose, working for the US Air Force, was able to find a link between the maximum of solar activity and the movement of the Sun about the common centre of mass of the solar system.

The work of Nelson and Jose was carried further by J. B. Blizard and H. P. Sleeper, both of whom undertook projects on solar-activity prediction on behalf of NASA. Blizard's work, undertaken in 1969, is particularly important to the theory of solar activity which I have developed over the last few years. She showed that when planets are in conjunction or opposition, as seen from the Sun, then there are violent storms on the Sun. The fact that some violent events on the Sun are associated with square positions of the planets, as seen from the Sun, puzzled Blizard. She concluded that no physical explanation was reasonable. This was because she was using equilibrium tidal theory in her work. Equilibrium tidal theory assumes that the height of the tide is directly proportional to the tidal tug of the planet. Her work was indicating that some form of resonance was occurring between the planets and the Sun. If the Sun, at certain times in the solar cycle, had magnetic oscillations the natural frequencies of which were equal to the tidal frequencies of some of the planets, then resonant amplification would occur. Close to resonance squares between certain planets would then play a part; in other words, when the tuning between the magnetic vibrations of the Sun and the tidal tug of the planets is close then angles of 90 degrees also become important. My own theory shows how this can occur.

Moving the Sun

Contrary to popular belief, the Sun is not fixed at the centre of the solar system. The planets, especially the larger outer planets like Jupiter, Saturn, Uranus and Neptune, move the Sun very slightly around the common centre of mass of the solar system. According to the theory I have developed, the changes in this movement of the Sun result in changes in the overall pattern of heat convection in the convective zone of the Sun. The convective motions are responsible for the generation of the solar magnetic field, and the changes in these motions result in a change of direction of this field. The evidence to support this part of the theory comes from the correlations discovered by Paul Jose.

Since the Sun's equator is moving faster than the rest of it, the magnetic lines of force of the Sun get wound up into structures that resemble magnetic canals as the solar cycle builds to a maximum. In 1845 the Astronomer Royal, George Biddell Airy, worked out a theory for hypothetical water canals running right around the Earth parallel to the equator. He showed that such canals could greatly amplify the tidal heights due to the Sun and Moon. I applied Airy's canal theory to the magnetic structures on the Sun. As a result of this work I was able to show that these structures make it possible for all the planets in turn to have an effect on violent outbursts of magnetic energy on the Sun. They do so because as the lines of force are stretched, so their periods of vibration change, and they are successively in tune with each of the tidal frequencies of the planets, starting with Mercury and ending with Neptune. In other words, the magnetic canals resonantly amplify the weak tidal tug of the planets, but the dominant planet at each stage of the solar cycle will be different. If the 'tuning' of the solar magnetic field lies between the periods of two planets, then square configurations of these two bodies will give rise to violent activity on the Sun. At other times conjunctions and oppositions will give rise to similar events. This theory is thus consistent with the findings of Blizard.

The Solar Wind and the Magnetic Field of Earth

Already in the last century it had been noticed that solar activity modulates the magnetic field of Earth. We now know why this is so. The Sun's magnetic activity modulates the solar wind, and it is this modulation which eventually modulates the magnetic field of the Earth. It is thus not surprising that the basic frequencies of the solar cycle manifest themselves in the variations of the geomagnetic record as obtained by geomagnetic observatories on the surface of the Earth. This is clear from the work of the geophysicists Robert Currie and F. de Meyer. Their mathematical analysis of long runs of geomagnetic recordings has also revealed that the response of the geomagnetic field to the modulations of the solar wind is far from simple. In other words, it has been found that not only are the basic frequencies of the solar cycle present in the geomagnetic record, but there are also multiples of these frequencies (these multiples of the basic frequency are called harmonics) in the record, and each well-defined frequency is flanked by several other very closely related frequencies. I am proposing that these arise in the following way.

The modulation of the geomagnetic field by the solar wind also manifests itself in the solar daily magnetic variation. This particular type of fluctuation of the Earth's field consists of periods of twenty-four hours, twelve hours and eight hours. If these frequencies were 'pure' then they would appear as narrow lines in a scan of the geomagnetic record. When one is tuning a radio receiver by turning the tuning knob, one passes through the 'lines' associated with different radio stations. However, even in this case, the lines have a finite width, in that it is possible to pick up a station, though not very clearly, on either side of the line associated with it. The lines of the solar daily magnetic variation also have finite widths, which are produced as follows. The daily distortion of the magnetosphere by the solar wind can be considered to be a special type of magnetic wave (called a transverse Alfvén wave) propagating around the Earth and concentrated mainly in the ionized gases of the Van Allen radiation belts which surround the Earth. Since these belts resemble doughnuts, they have finite thickness with different inner and outer radii. Since the Alfvén speed (the speed with which these waves travel) depends on the density of the gases and the strength of the field, and since both these quantities change with distance from the Earth, the angular speed of these waves will spread about the angular speed with which the Earth is spinning on its own axis with respect to the Sun. This will give rise to a finite width for the basic solar daily magnetic variation and for each of the harmonics associated with this variation.

Direct Planetary Effects on Geomagnetic Variations

We have already seen that certain planetary configurations have an effect on the solar cycle, and that, through the agency of the solar wind, these effects manifest themselves in the geomagnetic record. I am further proposing that the tidal tug of the planets has another, more direct, effect on geomagnetic variations. Since the mean planetary days are very close to the mean solar day, some of the many waves propagating through the Van Allen radiation belts will have the same angular speed as the planetary tides (due to gravitation), and, as a consequence of resonance, they will become phase-locked to these tides. I like to think of this as the magnetospheric equivalent of a laser. The distortion of the magnetosphere by the solar wind is doing the pumping, whereas the planetary tides are causing coherent phase-locking of some of the Alfvén waves.

There is a very well-known and well-researched variation of the geomagnetic field, which is connected with the Moon and is known as the lunar daily magnetic variation. The Moon does not only cause tides in the oceans, it also causes tides in the atmosphere, including the upper atmosphere, which consists of ionized gases. The electric currents generated in these gases by the tidal tug of the Moon give rise to associated magnetic fields, and these give rise to the lunar daily magnetic variation. Although the tides in the upper atmosphere are responsible for the major part of this variation, there is a small contribution from the electric currents generated in the salty water of the oceans by the oceanographic tides. The amplitude of the lunar daily magnetic variation is modulated by the phases of the Moon and by the solar cycle, but the basic period is very stable.

Resonance, Harmonics, Predictability and Chaos

Over the last few years a new branch of applied mathematics has been developing very rapidly. This field of research is called chaos theory and it has applications in a wide variety of fields – physics, astronomy, meteorology, biology and economics. For many years scientists in a variety of fields have been using mathematical models in their attempts to predict all sorts of phenomena, from planetary motions to economic developments. In order to solve the many mathematical equations that crop up in such models, in a reasonable length of time and within the constraints placed on them by the computing and calculating techniques available, it was necessary to start with the simplest assumptions. The simplest of all the many assumptions that one can make is that the effects produced by certain causes are always directly proportional to the causes. In other words, the response of any system to an outside influence is directly proportional to the amplitude of the influence, so if the amplitude is doubled the response would be twice as large, and if the amplitude is reduced by 40 per cent then the response will be reduced by 40 per cent. Technically this type of response is called a linear response, and one that does not conform to this principle is called a non-linear response. If a system has a completely linear response then one can predict its future development with absolute certainty. However, it has recently become clear that hardly any system, in the real world, conforms to the linear approximation. This means that systems which we have considered to be completely predictable have times when their behaviour verges on the chaotic, or is completely chaotic. It should be made clear that the use of the term chaos in this context differs from its normal use. Generally the term chaos is taken to mean a lack of order, which could arise from random events that have no pattern either in the frequencies or in the times of their occurrence. In the present context chaos arises when the main effect of a given cause generates side-effects which alter or interfere with it. We can illustrate this by considering the simple pendulum.

It has always been assumed that the simple pendulum, with a mass at the end of a piece of string, is a good example of a linear system. If the pendulum is displaced from its equilibrium position, then the force acting on it will be directly related to how far it has been displaced. This is strictly only true if the displacement is small in comparison with the length of the pendulum. Such a pendulum will have a natural period of swing. If we start to push the pendulum regularly, with a period equal to its natural period, then resonance will occur, and the amplitude of the swing will gradually increase with time. As the amplitude builds up we get to a situation in which the pendulum is no longer a linear system. When this happens the pendulum no longer has a simple period of swing, as harmonics of the basic period also begin to be present. The presence of these harmonics can at certain times reduce the amplitude to a value where it is once again valid to use the linear approximation. If we continue to apply the external push, then there will be another increase in the amplitude, and the process will be repeated. During the times when harmonics are present it becomes virtually impossible to predict the motion of the pendulum, and even relatively small changes in the initial starting conditions will give very different results. This means that there is a limited period of time in which we can predict the motion of a pendulum with a given set of starting conditions. Although the system is one which can be described as deterministic, in that we know the equations that describe its motion, nevertheless there are limits to the length of time in which we can, with certainty, predict what it will do. This limit has been called the predictability horizon. Is there a predictability horizon that is relevant to astrology? Let us look at the possibilities.

Chaos in Astronomy and Geomagnetism

The dynamics of the solar system presents a non-linear problem for astronomy. The planets are not only attracted by the Sun, they also attract each other, since they are governed by the laws of motion and the law of gravitation. This mutual attraction between the planets causes small changes in their orbits, called perturbations. These have to be taken into account when making long-term predictions. However, because the Sun is so much more massive than any of the other planets, these perturbations have only rather small effects on most terrestrial phenomena. The perturbations of the Earth's orbit by the other planets cause slight modulations of long-term climate, over several thousands of years.

In 1989 Jacques Laskar, working at the Bureau des Longitudes in Paris, carried out some calculations in an attempt to answer a very old question, 'Will the planets remain in their present orbits for all time?' His calculations seem to suggest that the orbits of the planets are chaotic, but on a time-scale of 100 million years. The source of this chaotic behaviour is still uncertain, but the suggestion has been made that it arises from resonances between the secular periods of the inner planets. Since the time-scales involved are so very long, this source of chaos can be of no importance in any theory of astrological causation.

The effects of the planets on the solar cycle are, according to the theory of tidal magnetic resonance, non-linear because the outer planets (Jupiter, Saturn, Uranus and Neptune) affect the Sun in two quite distinct ways, and because we are dealing with resonance. Thus at times there may well be periods when correlation between planetary alignments and solar activity appears to be chaotic. Our initial work on this problem seems to suggest that this may occur at the very peak of the solar cycle, within a month or two of the maximum, but we will need to investigate more complex mathematical models before the question can be answered. The chaotic behaviour seems, on the basis of our present calculations, to manifest itself on time-scales of between 150 and 200 years. This too may well be changed as we investigate other models.

The presence of harmonics of the solar cycle in the geomagnetic record seems to suggest that the response of the geomagnetic field to the solar wind is non-linear, as one would expect for such a complex interaction. This would explain why there is sometimes not a strict one-to-one correspondence between violent events on the Sun and geomagnetic storms, but it would also explain why geomagnetic storms increase in frequency as the solar cycle builds up to a maximum. This means that despite the development of chaotic behaviour well into the solar cycle, there are long-term correlations between solar activity and geomagnetic activity. This seems to be a general feature of chaotic behaviour. This point was well made by Anita Killian: 'It does not seem to matter where we look. If we peer deep enough into the laws governing motion we will find chaos. Likewise, within the kingdom of chaos one finds embedded the rule of higher order and regularity. It is the harmony of the spheres manifesting itself in ways more intricate than ever before imagined.'

We also need to look at the possibility of chaotic behaviour at the last interface of the theory – the interaction between human life and the geomagnetic field. Since, once again, the theory involves resonance, I call this part of the theory biomagnetic resonance. The full details of the theory, and the evidence on which it is based, are described in more detail in my book *Astrology: The Evidence of Science*.

Human Consequences of Biomagnetic Resonance

The branch of biological science known as behavioural genetics has produced some convincing evidence that some of our basic behavioural characteristics, which are associated with our personalities, are genetically inherited. The modern biophysical and biochemical approach to neural networks in the body attributes some behavioural characteristics to the way our nervous system is 'wired up'. I am proposing that the way our nervous system is connected up not only determines these basic character traits, but also determines the biological clock which will regulate the countdown to birth. This clock synchronizes itself, in the womb, to those fluctuations of the geomagnetic field which are locked in step with a particular planet. This means that planetary effects do not change what we have inherited but, in the case of a natural birth, the positions of the planets can 'label' those characteristics that we have inherited genetically from our parents by determining our time of birth. For further discussion of these points, again see my book *Astrology: The Evidence of Science*.

According to my theory we are all genetically tuned to receive a different set of melodies from the symphony which the planets, Sun and Moon are playing on the magnetic field of Earth. While in the womb, our familiar five senses are much less effective in receiving information than they are after we are born. However, the womb is no hiding-place from the all-pervading and constantly changing magnetic field of Earth, so the tunes which we pick up become part of our earliest memories. It is here that some of the magnetic music of the spheres becomes etched on our brains. The first role of our particular response to this music is to provide the musical cue for our entry on to the stage of the world. Thus the positions of the planets at our birth influence the personality characteristics which we have inherited genetically.

Astrological Forecasting

The scientific data to support the claim of many astrologers that they can predict the future in several ways is very sparse, and it largely takes the form of anecdotal evidence. Here we need to distinguish between two different types of event. First there are those events that do not involve human participation except, perhaps, as observers. These include geophysical and meteorological phenomena. It has already been seen that the occurrence of auroral lights far from the auroral oval is much more frequent when solar activity is high, and that this is related to specific planetary alignments. Geomagnetic storms – violent disruptions of the Earth's field which can affect the magnetic compass – are also more frequent when solar activity is high. Some scientists have found correlations between short-term weather and long-term climate and specific changes in the geomagnetic field, but these correlations are not as well established as the other links already mentioned. Other researchers have found connections between seismic activity, minute changes in the spin rate of Earth and solar activity, but these too are rather tenuous at the moment.

The second type of event does involve humans. There are two ways in which, according to the theory of biomagnetic tidal resonance, we can begin to understand human astrological forecasting. However, it should be emphasized that the evidence to support this speculative extension of the theory is still lacking.

Responding to Celestial Music

The first way in which the cosmos can play a part in tracing the future development of an individual is that we can use the positions of the planets at birth to identify his or her inherited personality characteristics, and from past experience of the development of people with these characteristics, we can sketch out future trends in their lives. There is thus no continuing effect of the geomagnetic field on the individual after birth, and the movements of the planets are then just the hands of a vast cosmic clock used to identify certain stages in that individual's development.

There is a second way in which the cosmos could play some part in the future development of individuals. The magnetic tunes recorded on our brains while we are still in the womb can become part of our earliest memories. When some of these tunes are played on the magnetic field of the Earth by the Sun, Moon and planets at a later stage in our lives, it could evoke these early memories, and hence it could influence the way we respond to a given situation. We are all familiar enough with the effect which different types of music can have on our moods or emotional responses to particular events, especially if certain pieces of music are associated with significant events in our lives, and it is as possible that the celestial magnetic music might have similar effects. However, such effects are likely to be more pronounced when the information coming to us via our senses is less effective; for example, in moments of revery or meditation, or when we are asleep. It is also likely that this recalling of the magnetic music from our memories can have some influence on our subsequent behaviour.

It is at this second level that the theory of chaos may, perhaps, play a part.

Astrological Predictability and Deterministic Chaos

The late John Addey, widely held by many astrologers to be the greatest British astrologer of the twentieth century, is the recognized founder of harmonic astrology. Using the data collected by Gauquelin, he shows that certain types of personality are associated, not with a particular harmonic of the Moon or with one of the planets, but with a set of harmonics which is related to the geocentric motions of these bodies. To illustrate his theory, Addey points out that there are two distinct types of sportsmen: one corresponding to the third harmonic of Mars and the other corresponding to the fourth harmonic of Mars. The presence of harmonics in the data points very clearly to a non-linear response that one would expect at, or near, resonant conditions. If this is indeed the case, then our responses to the magnetic music of the spheres would, on certain occasions, tend to be chaotic. The first-order mathematical model for biomagnetic tidal resonance does not at the moment allow precise calculations of the predictability horizon for this aspect of astrological forecasting, but the initial indications are that it will be roughly of the order of eleven or twelve years, which is close to the average period of the sunspot cycle.

The failure of astrological predictions is often trotted out by the critics of astrology as an indication that there can be no valid scientific basis for astrology. The theory of deterministic chaos shows that there could well be other reasons for this failure.

A few years ago the Royal Society organized a discussion meeting on predictability in science and society. One of the speakers at this meeting was the distinguished mathematician, Sir James Lighthill, FRS. In his lecture he introduced the idea of a predictability horizon:

I feel fully justified, therefore, in repeating that systems subject to the laws of Newtonian dynamics include a substantial proportion of systems that are chaotic; and that for these latter systems, there is no predictability beyond a finite predictability horizon. We are able to come to this conclusion without ever having to mention quantum mechanics or Heisenberg's uncertainty principle.

A fundamental uncertainty about the future is there, indeed, even on the supposedly solid basis of the good old laws of motion of Newton, which effectively are the laws of motion satisfied by all macroscopic systems. I have ventured to feel that this conclusion would be of interest to a discussion meeting on predictability in science and society. For example, there might be some other discipline where practitioners could be inclined to blame failures of prediction on not having formulated the right differential equations or on not employing a big enough computer to solve them precisely or on not using accurate initial conditions; yet we in mechanics know that, in many cases where the equations governing a system are known exactly and are solved precisely, nevertheless, however accurately the initial conditions may be observed, prediction is still impossible beyond a certain predictability horizon.

This is something which, I think, astrologers, and their critics, should keep in mind. The application of chaos theory to physics, meteorology, astronomy, biology and economics has made it quite clear that failures in attempts to predict the outcome of certain situations can arise from non-linear effects generating chaotic behaviour. Thus the failure of astrological predictions does not necessarily mean that causal mechanisms in this area do not exist, but it could indicate that the response of individuals to external cosmic factors is non-linear. This is just what one would expect near resonant conditions.

8 | Memories in Matter, Space and Time

We are surrounded by memories of the past. Above us, when we look at the night sky, we are seeing the universe as it was a long time ago. Beneath our feet we have the past fossilized in the rocks that have been laid down over aeons of time. The material of our bodies, indeed all the matter which we see, feel, smell, hear or taste, was brewed in the early universe, in stars and in the explosion of massive stars. There is no way that we can separate the present from the past history of the cosmos, our Milky Way galaxy, our Sun, the Earth and the evolution of life on Earth. In this chapter we will look at some of the memories that are present in matter, space and time.

Vapour Trails from Aircraft

The jet age has introduced us to the sight of vapour trails behind high-flying aircraft. These trails arise from the interaction of the gases ejected from the aircraft with the gases of the atmosphere. They give us information about where the aircraft has been. If the air is calm, and the aircraft is flying straight, then the trail is also straight, and it will remain for some time, perhaps drifting slowly across the sky. This means that it is a record of where the aircraft has been. However, each part of the trail was laid down at a slightly different time, so the trail could also be plotted in space-time where, once again, its world line will be a straight line. The principle of the vapour trail is made use of by physicists who investigate the structure and behaviour of subatomic particles.

Cloud and Bubble Chambers in Particle Physics

One of the first instruments to use the above principle is a device called the Wilson cloud or expansion chamber, named after its inventor C. T. R. Wilson. The expansion chamber causes condensation of a vapour into droplets along the path of a charged particle passing through a gas. The gas and vapour are contained in a cylinder with transparent windows, and the visible tracks are illuminated and photographed through the walls or top of the chamber. Condensation occurs as a result of a rapid expansion, which is produced by the controlled motion of a rubber diaphragm which forms one end of the cylinder. Such a chamber can be used in conjunction with a camera to record the motion of a charged particle which passes through the chamber. If, by means of a current-carrying coil of wire wrapped around the cylinder, a magnetic field is introduced into the chamber, then the particle will have a curved path. The radius of curvature of this trajectory is related to the strength of the field, the charge on the particle, its mass and its velocity. Hence, by combining the radius of curvature with other measurements, and knowing the strength of the magnetic field, it is possible to work out the masses of such particles.

The bubble chamber is an improved variation on the cloud chamber. Instead of using a supersaturated gas–vapour mixture it uses a superheated liquid. The passage of a charged particle through such a liquid may cause bubbles to grow along the track to a size at which they may be photographed before the start of the general boiling of the whole volume of the liquid. It is well known that the temperature at which a liquid such as water boils is related to the pressure applied to it. Thus water boils at a lower temperature at a high altitude than it will at sea level. In a bubble chamber a suitable liquid is heated above its normal boiling point and is maintained in the liquid phase by the application of suitable pressure. The pressure is then reduced by the movement of a piston or diaphragm and the liquid becomes overheated and sensitive to the presence of the ionization produced by the passage of a charged particle. After a few seconds general boiling will occur unless a re-compression prevents it. Photographs of the events which occur in cloud and bubble chambers are thus visible records and memories of the invisible events which happen on extremely short time-scales in the subatomic world. By examining those photographs we have an instantaneous recall of events that have occurred over a period of time, however brief.

On the Nature of Fossils

Fossils are petrified objects with the appearance of animal bones, shells, teeth, vegetable leaves and stalks. They were known from classical times, and were discussed by the philosopher Aristotle as well as by other classical scholars. Two scholars of the Renaissance, Conrad Gesner and Ulisse Aldrovandi, collected many of these objects, storing them in cabinets in museums. They also wrote several books, illustrated with woodcuts, which identified and described them.

In the seventeenth and eighteenth centuries fossils became a hotbed of scientific controversy. Some naturalists, for example Bernard Palissy, Robert Hooke and Nicolaus Steno, proposed that they were petrified animal and vegetable remains. They argued that these fossils might have infiltrated into solid rock by means of floods. Alternatively they might have become embedded in newly forming strata on the seabed, and over a long period of time they might have been solidified by the action of heat, compression and chemical forces.

A completely different point of view was put forward by Robert Plot and Athanasius Kircher, who held that these fossilized objects were produced by the same types of interatomic and intermolecular forces that produce crystals. The Neo platonic, Hermetic and Aristotelian philosophies of the Renaissance believed that living Nature, through 'plastic vertues', had the power to impose form on all matter, however low in the chain of being, but by the end of the seventeenth century these philosophies found few supporters.

It was at this time that the theory of fossils as organic remains became more popular. The study of fossils became important in the eighteenth and nineteenth centuries for two reasons. The first was the discovery that fossils are not distributed randomly throughout the crust of Earth. Crystalline rocks like granite were found to contain no fossils. Bedded rocks such as clays and limestone often contained large quantities of fossils. It was also discovered that certain types of fossil were found in distinctive bands of rock. A good example of this was the discovery that fossil ferns occurred in coal seams. In 1816 William Smith wrote the book *Strata Identified by Organized Fossils*, in which he showed how fossils could be used as indicators of strata type. This work made it possible, not only to identify rocks, but also to estimate their age from the absence or presence of fossils, and from the type and degree of complexity of the fossils found in them. By assessing whether fossils were terrestrial or marine, fresh-water or seawater, one could also find out about the physical origins of the rocks in which they were contained.

Fossils and the Evolution of Life

The first reason the study of fossils became important was thus largely, although not exclusively, geological. The second reason had much more to do with biology. The study of the location of fossils in a column of strata suggested to some naturalists, for example Buffon and de Luc, that life may have evolved through successive stages, finally leading to man. In the first half of the nineteenth century most geologists were convinced that the fossil record showed a pro-gression in the nature and complexity of living organisms. There was raging controversy at the time as to how this had happened. Georges Cuvier and Adam Sedgwick proposed that the extinction of certain species, like the dinosaurs, came about as the result of natural catas-trophes, but that the appearance of new species was the direct result of divine intervention. But in 1859, in his book *The Origin of Species*, Charles Darwin proposed the theory of gradual evolution by natural selection. However, he believed that the fossil record was too incom-plete and inadequate to use as positive evidence for his work. Plaus-ible evolutionary trees for the ancestry of some species, for example the horse, were traced by O. C. Marsh and T. H. Huxley, and this work strengthened the case for evolution.

The Presence of the Past

The memories we have discussed so far are imprints of the past which have been fossilized into matter over a period of time. By extracting core samples from rocks or the bed of the oceans, we have almost immediate access to past information in that the extraction of these cores and their analysis can be carried out in a period of time that is infinitesimal in comparison with the time-scales involved in their formation. Rupert Sheldrake, in his books *A New Science of Life* and *The Presence of the Past*, proposes a much more fundamen-tal and basic role for memory.

The essence of his theory is that memory is inherent in all natural phenomena. He proposes that all natural systems inherit a collective memory of their own kind and each system is shaped by 'morphic fields' containing a collective memory. For example, rabbits are not rabbit-shaped only because their DNA encodes their proteins, but also because there is a rabbit 'morphic field' that informs their growth and instinctive behaviour. Very important to Sheldrake's hypothesis is the concept of morphic resonance.

Morphic Resonance

In response to the question, 'how could such a memory possibly work?', Sheldrake supplies the following answer:

The hypothesis of formative causation postulates that it depends on a kind of resonance, called morphic resonance. Morphic resonance takes place on the basis of similarity. The more similar an organism is to previous organisms, the greater their influence on it by morphic resonance. And the more such organisms there have been, the more powerful their cumulative influence . . .

Morphic resonance differs from the kinds of resonance already known to science, such as acoustic resonance (as in the sympathetic vibration of stretched strings), electromagnetic resonance (as in the tuning of a radio set to a transmission at a particular frequency) . . . Unlike these kinds of resonance, morphic resonance does not involve a transfer of energy from one system to another, but rather a non-energetic transfer of information. However, morphic resonance does resemble the known kinds of resonance in that it takes place on the basis of rhythmic patterns of activity.

According to the hypothesis of formative causation, morphic resonance occurs between such rhythmic structures of activity on the basis of similarity, and through resonance past patterns of activity influence the fields of subsequent similiar systems. Morphic resonance involves a kind of action at a distance in both space and time. The hypothesis assumes that the influence does not decline with distance in space and time.

This last requirement echoes exactly what Bell's theorem tells us about quantum mechanics.

Bell's Theorem and Quantum Mechanics

Bell's theorem basically shows us that if quantum mechanics is valid (and all physical experiments have so far failed to reveal that this might not be so), then measurements made on two particles will always be correlated, no matter how far apart they are. This can be illustrated by using two subatomic particles. We have already mentioned that these particles spin on their own axes, rather as tops or planets do. Physicists call this property of particles their 'spin'. Suppose we have a two-particle system in which one particle is spinning in the opposite direction to the other, when they are very close together – this is normally referred to as the one particle having spin UP and the other particle spin DOWN. If we measure the spins of the particles after they have been separated by a large distance, then we find that the spins of the particles are still one UP and one DOWN.

Such particles, because of their spin, behave as if they were little magnets, so we say they have magnetic moments. It is possible to change their orientations by passing them through magnetic fields. Quantum mechanics tells us that if we change the orientation of one particle, so that instead of spinning UP about a vertical axis, it is now spinning LEFT about a horizon axis, then we will find that the other particle is also spinning about a horizontal axis, but in the opposite direction, which we will call RIGHT. These results of quantum mechanics have been confirmed by two experiments – the first one performed in 1972 by John Clauser and Stuart Freeman in America and the second by A. Aspect, P. Grangier and C. Roger at CERN, in Geneva, in 1981. Thus, remarkable though it may seem, there is some form of instantaneous communication between the two particles, such that changing the spin of the one instantaneously changes the spin of the other.

In *The Dancing Wu Li Masters*, Gary Zukav quotes the following statement made by the physicist Henry Stapp:

Quantum phenomena provide *prima facie* evidence that *information gets around in ways that do not conform to classical ideas*. Thus the idea that information is transferred superluminally is, a priori, not unreasonable ... Everything we know about nature is in accord with the idea that the fundamental processes of nature lie outside space-time but generate events that can be located in space-time. The theorem of this paper [Bell's paper] supports this view of nature by showing that superluminal transfer of information is necessary, barring certain alternatives ... that seem less reasonable. Indeed, the philosophical position of Bohr seems to lead to the rejection of the other possibilities and hence, by inference, to the conclusion that super-luminal transfer of information is necessary.

Implicate Order and Morphic Resonance

The physicist David Bohm has proposed that an 'implicate order' exists, and he uses this order to explain the strange behaviour of the quantum world. Sheldrake's book *The Presence of the Past* contains the following quote from Bohm, in which the possible relationship between the implicate order and morphic resonance is explored:

The implicate order can be thought of as a ground beyond time, a totality, out of which each moment is projected into the explicate order [which Bohm sees as the order of ordinary experience]. For every moment that is projected into the explicate order there would be another movement in which that moment would be injected or 'introjected' back into the implicate order. If you have a large number of repetitions of this process, you'll start to build up a fairly constant component to this series of projection and injection. That is, a fixed disposition would become established. The point is that, via this process, past forms would tend to be repeated or replicated in the present, and that is similar to what Sheldrake calls a morphogenetic field and morphic resonance.

Before discussing the relationship of the plasma space theory and the world-line web to Sheldrake's morphogenetic fields and Bohm's implicate order, it is first necessary to discuss the theory of cosmic transference.

The Theory of Transference

The theory of transference is often made use of in detective work to solve crimes. In its most basic form it says that a criminal will leave something of himself at the scene of the crime, and usually he will also, inadvertently, take something from the scene away with him; if he is caught he can quite often be connected with the scene in this way. For example, in addition to leaving fingerprints (if he did not wear gloves) on the objects he handled, he might also have picked up some wet mud on his shoes as he walked through the garden, and this mud could have picked up hairs from the carpet of the room in which he committed the crime. Traces of many different kinds of interaction can be important in the solution of a crime. If the criminal was injured at the scene of the crime, he may have shed some blood, which can be identified, or alternatively, if he injured the victim of his crime, he may have picked up some of the victim's blood.

We can extend this theory to physical interactions that take place in space and time. For any two subatomic particles to interact with each other, they either have to come into direct physical contact with each other at the same point of space at the same time, or they must get close enough to each other for their 'fields' to interact. In both cases the world lines of the particles will first converge and then, after the interaction, there will be one of several possibilities. First, if they repel each other in any way, their world lines will diverge. Second, if they attract each other, they could merge, and in this case their two world lines will become one after they have merged. Third, they may be moving so fast that the force of attraction is insufficiently strong to cause them to merge, in which case the world lines will diverge again. Fourth, the collision, or other interaction, might cause the particles to change into other particles, and in this case more than two particles will emerge from the encounter.

In the plasma space theory electrons and protons are shuttles which, with their trailing electrified plasma space bundles, have woven the past, are now weaving the present and will continue to weave the future. The part of the web which has already been woven is the memory bank of all past interactions, and the threads with which the present is being woven are all entwined in the past. This means that every thread of the present is instantaneously linked to all the threads with which it has interacted in the past, which covers the whole history of the universe. In the plasma space theory two interacting particles will both carry memory traces of the interaction. The strengths of the memories will depend on the type of interaction and its duration. Systems of particles can also interact with each other, and in the case of two particles, or two systems of particles, the longer and the closer the interaction, the greater will be the strength of the memories. It is possible for the particles, or the systems of particles, to communicate with each other after the inter-action, via this common memory. Intersections between world lines and branch points in space-time are important to the theory. The ability of two particles to 'communicate' via the world-line memory is clearer if their world lines have crossed, or if they share a branch point in space-time, and if there are no, or very few, crossings with other particles or systems between this common point in their world lines. These general ideas can be understood in more detail by applying them to some concrete examples.

Two-particle Interactions

We have already seen that the 'balls of yarn' of plasma space which form the cores of the proton and the electron are spinning on their own axes, and hence these particles will behave like little magnets with their own spin and magnetic moment. Spin is also called angular momentum. To find the angular momentum of a single particle spinning about an axis, we have to multiply its ordinary momentum (which is its speed multiplied by its mass) by the distance the particle is from the axis. Angular momentum is always conserved in physical systems. Thus if we were to change the distance of the particle from the axis, then the speed with which it is moving would also change: if the distance were increased, the speed would decrease, and vice versa. This point is well illustrated by the spinning of an ice skater. If he starts spinning with his arms outstretched and then lowers his arms, he will begin to spin faster. With the arms outstretched there is a certain angular momentum, which will be conserved, and therefore as the arms are brought closer to the spin axis, the body will inevitably spin faster.

If two subatomic particles have the same mass, and originate at the same point of space at the same time, but one is spin UP and the other spin DOWN, then, as we have already seen, quantum mechanics tells us that they will retain these correlations no matter how far apart they are. According to the plasma space theory, this is because they are still connected by the world-line web, and angular momentum can be transmitted instantaneously between two such particles. In other words, if some of the fibre bundles of the web are twisted at one point, then this twisting will be communicated immediately to another part of the web, provided there is a 'clear' channel between the two parts, i.e. they share a branch point in space-time. For large bodies and collections of particles this will in general not be the case, because they are composed of particles that have had more complex histories and hence the channel will be noisy, and the communication will not be very clear. It is for this reason that, according to plasma space theory, it would not be possible to develop a system of communication using the instantaneous transfer of angular momentum between parts of the world-line web.

The Wave-like Nature of Electrons

We have already looked at the interference that can take place between different sets of waves; we saw that Polynesian navigators can use interference between incoming ocean waves and waves reflected by the coast, and the distortion of these two sets by islands, to find their way around the islands. The interference of two sets of waves sent out from radio transmitters has also been used by the navigators of ships to find their way around the oceans of the world. Interference was used by the physicist Thomas Young to establish the wave nature of light. He passed light from a source through a single slit to produce a coherent set of waves, and then passed this light through two further slits before allowing the combined light to fall on a screen. The light waves from the two slits interfered with each other to produce a set of light and dark bands on the screen. A light band would be produced when the peaks and troughs of the waves, coming via the two slits, were in phase, and strengthened each other, and a dark band would be produced when the peaks and troughs were out of phase, and cancelled each other out. This experiment demonstrated the wave nature of light.

An experiment similar to Young's twin-slit experiment has been used to establish the wave nature of electrons. In a vacuum the electrons from a filament were passed through two slits before being allowed to fall on a screen. The pattern produced on the screen resembled that produced by Young's slits in the case of light, thus showing that, under certain circumstances, electrons behaved as if they were waves. When there was only one slit, then the electrons behaved as if they were particles, and formed a rather fuzzy line on the screen about the direction which passed from the filament through the single slit. In other words, most of the electrons passed through the slit in straight lines, as particles would, but a few did spread out after passing through, as one would expect if they retained some of their wavelike properties. The result of this experiment can be understood in terms of the world-line web.

The evolution and recycling of matter means, as we have already stated, that the whole of space is criss-crossed by the web. As electrons move through space, they will undergo frequent collisions with the web, thus setting it vibrating. The electrons will also pick up some of the natural vibrations of the web. This is rather like a speedboat moving through the sea, which not only creates its own waves but also responds to the natural waves of the ocean. The de Broglie wavelength of an electron depends on its momentum, and it is this wavelength that determines the dimensions of the interference pattern which it will produce in a twin-slit experiment. The interaction of the waves produced by the motion of the electron and the natural oscillations of the web gives rise to a group of waves, the group velocity of which is equal to the velocity of the electron. When both slits are open then the electrons passing through the two slits will give rise to waves in the world-line web which will interfere with each other, and this interference informs the electron where to go on the screen. The phase velocity of waves along the web can be greater than the speed of light, as required by Bohm's quantum potential and de Broglie's matter waves.

The World-line Web and Morphogenetic Fields

The world-line web contains information on past interactions of particles and groups of particles. Every specific grouping of a number of different particles will have its own natural vibrations, and these natural vibrations can interact with electromagnetic vibrations of the same frequency if they are available in the neighbourhood of the particle. It is this principle that can be used to identify atoms and molecules using spectroscopic analysis. According to the plasma space theory, it is possible for identical collections of particles to resonate with each other via the world-line web, and this would be the basis of Sheldrake's morphic resonance. However, this theory would claim that small amounts of energy transfer can take place via the world-line web, and the amounts available will on the whole have to be shared by the entire web, so except where there are clear channels linking the sets of identical particles, the amounts will be weakened by space and time. If, however, the world lines of the one set have interacted with those of the other set, and they share several branch points in space and time, then this will increase the possibility of morphic resonance between the two sets. The branch points will thus act like a space-time telephone exchange between the two sets or groups of particles.

The genes of living organisms can act as space-time telephone exchanges, through which information on structure, form, development and instinctive behaviour can be passed on from one generation to the next, via clear channels, in the world-line web. This part of the plasma space theory would thus support Sheldrake's statements that the 'more similar an organism is to a previous organism, the greater their influence on it by morphic resonance. And the more such organisms there have been, the more powerful their cumulative influence.'

It seems to me, however, that his statement that 'the hypothesis [of formative causation] assumes that this influence does not decline in space and time' should be modified on the basis of the world-line memory-bank model. In this model his statement holds true, provided there is a clear channel of world-line threads, such as one would have as a result of linking space-time gene telephone exchanges together. As it stands, this aspect of the hypothesis seems to me to lead us into some difficulties, out of which we can be helped by a modification along the lines I propose.

Some Difficulties with Sheldrake's Morphogenetic Fields and Morphic Resonance

There are several difficulties that I encountered when I attempted to understand Sheldrake's theory in the way in which he proposed it. However, there are three specific ones which I would like to mention at this point.

It seems to me that, as it stands, his theory makes possible the spontaneous generation of life on Earth. Provided we have the right collection of basic chemicals, it should be possible for these chemicals to form into a basic life form spontaneously as a result of morphic resonance, especially if the effects of these fields do not diminish with distance in time and space. It is well known, however, that no spontaneous generation of life has been observed to occur on the surface of the Earth.

The fact that certain biological species, for example dinosaurs, are now extinct, also presents a problem for the theory. If extinction took place as a result of a short-term change in the environment, as some people believe, then a return to the original conditions should give rise, through morphic resonance, to the reappearance of the species. This too has not been observed.

Sheldrake has also suggested that these fields can aid the learning process, in that ideas can be transmitted via the morphogenetic fields. For more than twenty years I have been involved in education, at a variety of levels, and I have found no convincing evidence that large classes learn new ideas more easily than small ones, even when the class contains some people who respond to new ideas very quickly.

The world-line-web concept provides a means of overcoming these difficulties. According to this concept, communication via the web is strongest if there are clear channels between the present and specific branch points in space-time. For living organisms the gene telephone exchanges act as very strong branch points. It is accepted by most scientists that life on Earth started with a single organism – so this was the branch point for all life, to which we all have genetic connections of different degrees of clarity. Extinction of a species, for any reason, leads to the termination of the 'chain of gene telephone exchanges' for that species. Although all human life will share a common branch point, this branch point is a long way in the past, and so communication through it will be very weak. The ability to communicate via a common gene telephone exchange becomes stronger as we move to groups whose members have world lines that ran closer together for relatively long periods of time. Thus it is strengthened by racial similarities and family ties, and it should be extremely strong in the case of identical twins.

In this chapter we have looked at a variety of different types of memory. We also discussed, briefly, the ideas of Rupert Sheldrake and David Bohm and the relationship between their ideas, as well as the relationship of their ideas to the concept of the world-line web of memory. In the next chapter we shall explore the evidence for such a memory which we can get from identical twins.

9 | The Evidence from Twins

Our hearts, my love, were form'd to be
The genuine twins of Sympathy,
  They live with one sensation:
In joy or grief, but most in love,
Like chords in unison they move,
  And thrill with like vibration.

Thomas Moore, 'Sympathy: To Julia'

In this chapter we will explore the application of some of the concepts developed in previous chapters to the understanding of the strange links between twins. Although the major part of the chapter will be devoted to identical twins we will also briefly look at non-identical and astrological twins. We will, however, start with some examples which seem to indicate that identical twins may well have extrasensory ways of communicating with each other, or, alternatively, that their lives have strangely identical ways of developing in time.

My own interest in the phenomenon of twins started with a local example. A colleague has related to me several instances when he seemed able to communicate with his twin brother who now lives and works in America. Here I will quote just two of the cases he told me about. On one occasion his brother felt a strong urge to go into a church, in America, for silent prayer, and as he went into the church, he noted the time. At that same instant, according to Greenwich Mean Time (now called Universal Time), my colleague was here in England, at the bedside of their mother, who had just died.

On another occasion, he was captaining a ship crossing the Indian Ocean at night, when he spotted another ship from the bridge. He felt the urge to contact this ship by radio, and when he did so it was his brother who replied.

Another interesting case of a rather strange encounter between identical twins, which also has a nautical flavour, concerns the McWhirter brothers, Norris and Ross, who together created *The Guinness Book of Records*. Both of them joined the Royal Navy and reached the rank of sub-lieutenant. They then joined the crews of two different minesweepers: Norris was detailed to one in Singapore and Ross went to one in the Mediterranean. These ships went on separate voyages to Valletta, in Malta, and collided just before getting there.

Twins – Strange Similarities

There are several puzzling coincidences between identical twins that have been separated at birth. Sheila and Jacqueline Lewis were adopted at birth by different families and neither of them knew that they were one of a pair of identical twins until twenty-six years later. Both of them were admitted on the same day in June 1976 to Southmead Hospital in Bristol, England, suffering from the same rare skin disease. The disease was a hereditary one and so it was not surprising that it should affect both sisters, since identical twins are monozygotic – they come from a single fertilized egg that divides into two in the womb, and so have an identical set of genes. It is the other similarities that are surprising. By chance they were put in the same treatment room, and it was here that they soon discovered they were twins. They also shared many physical similarities, as one would expect. Both had double-jointed little fingers, both had birth-marks on their necks, both had moles on their left knees, both had had kidney trouble and both had suffered from pain in their left leg for several years.

The 'Jim twins' from Ohio, USA, provide us with another example. They were reunited in 1979, thirty-nine years after they had been separated at birth by adoption. They had many surprising non-physical similarities. They both had dogs, whom they named Troy; they both had the same first names – James Springer and James Lewis; and both of them had worked as attendants at filling stations before working for the same hamburger chain. They also had the same hobbies – technical drawing and carpentry. At very nearly the same stage of their lives they had had extremely similar patterns in their migraine headaches, and for both of them this ailment stopped at the same time. Both of them had been married twice, the first time to women called Linda and the second time to women called Betty. They also both drove Chevrolets and took their holidays at the same time of year on the same stretch of beach in Florida.

Synchronicity and Twins

A particularly strange example of synchronization between identical twins occurred at 4.35 p.m. on a Saturday in July 1948. At this time Alice Lamba was reading in the parlour of her home in Springfield, Illinois, USA, when she suddenly felt a jolt on the left side of her body. This was followed by a feeling of shock and a sharp stabbing pain in her side. She then seemed to be knocked off her chair by some unseen force, and just before fainting, she said, 'Something's happened to Dianne.' At that very instant, seventy miles away, Dianne, her twin, was travelling on a train that had just been derailed, and she had been thrown across the carriage. When she woke up in hospital, it was to find that she had suffered severe concussion, and that she had fractured two ribs. Alice also complained of pains in her side, and when she was X-rayed it turned out that she had fractured the same two ribs.

Another example of synchronized injuries in identical twins is provided by the sisters Nita Hust and Nettie Porter. Nettie was involved in a car crash in Roseville, California, on 21 July 1975. When this happened, Nita, who worked in a hospital four hundred miles away, suffered pains down her left leg. She was surprised to find, on rolling up her trousers, bruises working their way up her leg. The spontaneous development of her marks, which were very similar to those on her sister's leg, was witnessed by the matron at the hospital.

A third example comes from *Parallels: A Look at Twins*, by Ted Wolner and Harvey Stein. Apparently the identical twin of a young woman was suffering from acute appendicitis, and she relates the following story: 'When they came to tell me this, they found me on the floor in pain. When the doctors took her into the surgery, I could tell the moment when they started cutting and when they sewed her up. I was in the waiting-room with my mother who said, "The operation should be over by now," and I said, "No, mother, the doctor has just started." And, indeed, the doctor later verified that the operation had been delayed.'

Giving Birth Together

There have been several instances of twin sisters giving birth to children at very nearly the same time. In 1974 Jennifer Vickers and Patricia Harlow gave birth within hours, and on 15 January 1975 Yvonne Gale and Maureen Smith both gave birth at Kingston Hospital in Surrey, England, within 23 minutes of each other. The non-identical twin daughters, Anita and Vera, of Otto Heise of Einbeck in West Germany, were unlike in character and looks, but they were delivered of babies at the same moment in the same clinic. Geraldine and Jackie, twin daughters of the Herz family, had babies within days of each other on no less than twelve occasions.

Dying Together

In November 1970 Finnish twin girls of twenty-three died within minutes of each other in a small village in Finland, for no obvious medical reason. Within a short while the news had spread around the world. As pointed out by Dr J. B. Rhine, a well-known investigator into paranormal phenomena, if anything like this happens to twins, then it is more newsworthy than if it had happened to any other pair of closely related people. He went on to say: 'One of the firm facts about it . . . is that it indicates that the medical sciences have much yet to discover about the nature of life and death, and that two individuals can live and die almost as one.'

The Aller twins from Morganton, North Carolina, provide an even better documented parallel to the Finnish case. These two women died at the age of thirty-two in a state mental hospital, in April 1962. They had been sent to the hospital because they had been diagnosed as suffering from schizophrenia. The twins were separated in the hospital, because of problems with medication, despite their strong desire that they should be allowed to stay together. During the first night they died, almost at the same time, in different wards, and when they were discovered they were crouched in the same foetal position. The post-mortem revealed no apparent medical cause of death.

Some other cases have also been reported in which one of the twins has died a violent death, and the other has died almost simultaneously, apparently in sympathy but with no actual sensory transmission of knowledge concerning the other's death. Such a story was told by Mrs Joyce Crominski to the Australian magazine *Truth*. She had had twin sisters Helen and Peg. One night, three quarters of an hour before midnight, Peg was killed in a car crash when the steering

wheel penetrated her chest. At the same time Helen woke up scream-
ing, saying she had a severe pain in her chest. On her way to the
hospital, she died in the ambulance.

Pain Transference in Non-identical Twins

There have also been reports of pain transference between non-identical twins. Christopher Gool suffered severe pains in his stomach
when his twin sister gave birth, although they were separated by
three hundred miles. On another occasion Yvonne fell over and had
to go to hospital to have her arm injuries treated, when Christopher,
who is a policeman, hurt his arm in a brawl. When the non-identical
twin of Martha Burke of California was burned to death in a plane
crash in the Canary Islands in 1977, she herself suffered severe pains
in her chest and stomach. When the brother of Mrs Sheargold
cracked a rib, she felt his pain, although they were miles apart, and
when she suffered a leg injury, her brother was kept awake by the
pain.

Dubious Investigations of Twins

Some of the supposedly convincing results concerning large samples
of twins contain material that is open to doubt, and the results are
thus either of limited validity, or totally invalid. This, unfortunately,
has happened on more than one occasion.

Sir Cyril Burt, the father of British educational psychology, published, in 1966, the results of forty-five years of research, on what
was supposed to be the most extensive sample ever studied of twins
that had been separated at birth. This sample, he claimed, consisted
of fifty-three pairs of identical twins. It now seems very unlikely that
he could have had access to such a large sample, and much of his
work may have been pure invention, constructed to prove the points
which he wished to make. The bulk of his papers was lost when a
German bomb destroyed part of the records office of University
College, London; some of the work, it was claimed, had been carried
out with two assistants called Miss Conway and Miss Howard, but
there are no records of these assistants. Because of these doubts
about his claims Burt's work is of no value at all, in spite of his
having been previously a highly respected psychologist.

In 1937 Newman, Freeman and Holzinger, working in Chicago, studied nineteen cases which were supposed to show that heredity played a bigger role in achievement than other factors. It now seems likely, however, that they had carefully selected subjects who were very similar to start with. In the study conducted by Dr James Shields in London in 1962, some of the twins had been looked after by different members of the same family, and they could not really be treated as completely separate.

The Psychic Powers of Twins

Professor J. B. Rhine posed the question 'Do identical twins have any special means of coordinating their activities that others do not?' To this question he gives a yes and no answer. He reported on a recent study which compared the clairvoyant card-guessing ability of identical and clairvoyant twins, pointing out that although the identical twins did marginally better, the results were not really statistically significant. He concluded, 'Since the entire group showed evidence of this ability, all that can be said is that identical twins are as good as fraternal twins, and that is the indication from all other sources.'

The phenomenon of identical twins thinking the same thoughts at the same time is one that has often been reported. But telepathic communication between twins seems very elusive in a formal laboratory setting. While investigating the twins Nettie and Nita, Dr David Lykken, of the University of Minnesota, discovered that when Nita or Nettie concentrated on the other twin, then the other twin soon telephoned. This is rather difficult to investigate in the controlled setting of a laboratory. An experiment to do something similar, in a controlled environment, was carried out by Drs Duane and Behrendt. These investigators wired up a pair of identical twins, to record their brainwave patterns, in separate rooms. Their results provided no convincing proof for the hypothesis. In the first experiment they found that a stimulus given to the brain of one twin was received by the other twin, simultaneously. However, when they investigated sixteen other pairs of twins, only one pair responded in a similar way.

Professor Thomas Bouchard, also of the University of Minnesota, USA, investigated a much more detailed sample. By giving a great deal of publicity to his planned project, he managed to find more than thirty cases of identical twins who had been separated very early in life, and were not reunited until they had grown up. Bouchard and his team found many physical, intellectual and behavioural similarities between these sets of twins. The investigations by Bouchard and Lykken led them to suggest that many twins possess a strong telepathic link, although this does not always show up convincingly in controlled laboratory experiments.

The Clock of Life Theory

Since 1953, Professor Luigi Gedda and a colleague at the Gregor Mendel Institute in Rome have investigated the case histories of large numbers of twins, and added to their data bank by directly investigating as many new pairs of twins as were willing to take part in the project. From this investigation Gedda formulated the 'Clock of Life' hypothesis. He proposed that both twins of a pair have identical clocks, which tick in perfect synchronization with each other. These clocks cannot be simple clocks, in that they also include scheduled instructions, which can play a part in 'programming' some of the behavioural patterns of each member of the pair. This concept very naturally links up with the much more general subject of biological clocks and with astrology.

Astrological Twins

Astrological twins are people of the same sex, born at the same time, who are not related in any way, but who nevertheless have surprising parallels in their lives. There is a very brief mention of this subject by Derek and Julia Parker in their *The New Complete Astrologer*. Apparently Julia Parker was born within an hour of David Blair – the internationally known ballet dancer – and about 125 miles from his birthplace. As children they both studied ballet, and went to specialized schools at an early age. They also both taught ballet, they were married within weeks of each other and they live about a mile apart. The Parkers go on to say, 'Comparison of the lives of astrological twins is an absorbing field of study; several known cases reveal similarities in personal mannerisms, marriage partners – even the choice of a rug to decorate the home!'

A few other interesting examples have also surfaced. Two Goran Lundbergs were born at the same time in Sweden, and both men won scholarships to study in the USA in 1966. Bethany College in Lingsborg, Kansas, was the educational institute at which they both chose to study, and this was where they met.

Jacquelin Luscher and Elizabeth Boxxhard were also born on the same day in the same Swiss town. They were then separated at birth, but their lives followed similar patterns. Their weddings took place on the same day, and both women moved to Los Angeles at the same time. On the same day they both gave birth to girls, attended by the same doctor, in the same hospital, which was where and how they met each other.

Planetary Twins

'Planetary twins' are those born, not at the same time, but with the same planet in similar sectors of the sky. The evidence for such 'twins' comes from the works of Michel and Françoise Gauquelin. The first positive result obtained by the Gauquelins related to the births of 576 members of the French Academy of Medicine. These doctors had obtained academic distinction as a result of their research work. They were selected by these researchers from medical directories and, to avoid bias, they used objective criteria for this selection process. Theoretically these people could have been born at any time of the day, yet these medical men tended to be born when Mars or Saturn had just risen, or had passed the highest point in the sky. In a further experiment they used a different set of 508 doctors, and came up with the same results.

Exhaustive studies by the Gauquelins of many different groups of people who had obtained success in their various professions led them to the following conclusions. Saturn in the positions previously mentioned was associated with much higher than average frequencies of births of scientists and physicians, but on the other hand much lower frequencies of birth for actors, journalists, writers and painters. Few scientists and physicians were born under Jupiter, but more than the average number of actors, playwrights, politicians, military leaders, top executives and journalists were born under the planet. For Mars the high-frequency groups were physicians, military leaders, sports champions and top executives, whereas the low frequency groups were painters, musicians and writers.

The Planetary Effect

The Gauquelins also found that if a child was born with a particular planet in a specific area of the sky, then it was more than likely that at least one of the parents would have been born with the same planet in a similar part of the sky. This effect obeyed the established laws of heredity, did not hold when birth was medically induced and was enhanced by disturbances of the geomagnetic field. Since my research over the last twenty years has been on magnetic fields in celestial objects, I decided to see how I could use my knowledge to explain these findings of Gauquelin. The result is the theory described in Chapter 7. This theory is also able to explain some of the synchronistic behaviour of identical twins.

Biomagnetic Tidal Resonance and Twins

In this theory the neural network, as we have already seen, is wired up on the instructions of the genetic code. This wiring up is what determines the personality characteristic of the individual. It also determines the rate of ticking of the internal biological clocks of a person, and the frequencies of the geomagnetic field to which the individual will respond. Identical twins have the same genetic make-up so they have the same biological clocks, ticking at the same rate, and they will have very similar personalities. This means that the particular variations of the geomagnetic field to which they respond will be the same, and these frequencies will synchronize the ticking of their biological clocks. The 'tunes' and 'melodies' which they receive from the solar-system symphony being played on the magnetic field of Earth by the Sun, Moon and planets will be the same, and if they are both listening to this 'music' at the same time, it is very likely that they may respond in similar ways. I did, however, point out that in later life this 'music' probably only plays a part when we are meditating, or in moments of revery, so if one twin is listening to the music, then that twin might respond in a particular way, but if the other twin is not listening then he will not respond in the same way. This theory may be able to explain some examples of synchronized behaviour, but it is not able to explain all such examples. For example, it cannot explain the transference of sensory collected knowledge from one twin to the next, nor can it explain the transference of pain, injury or death. Some other agency must be involved. I believe this agency to be resonant communications via the world-line web of memory.

Identical Twins and the World-line Web of Memory

In terms of the world-line web, the world lines of identical twins would have had the same origin in space and time, and for a full nine months these world lines would have run on parallel paths that were very close together. At the end of the nine months, their world lines would have diverged only slightly if they were brought up together by their parents in the same house and went to the same school. If they were separated at birth their world lines would have diverged much more, but in the world-line-web theory of matter and its evolution, such world lines would still be linked together by their past interactions. In other words, the branch point is fossilized in the past in the moment of conception, and during the period of gestation. Just as subatomic particles can communicate via their world-line web, under certain circumstances, so twins have a limited means of communication via their world lines. Although there is no way of breaking the world lines that link us to the past, the clarity of these lines as channels of information is weakened by the number of interactions we have with other people. Thus in the case of identical twins not separated at birth, these world lines as channels of communication will be clearer than they will be in the case of identical twins that were separated close to birth. This type of communication will also be open to non-identical twins, because although they do not have the same genetic make-up, they nevertheless have world lines that have run very close together for nine months.

The Noise and the Signal

Radio engineers and scientists often talk about the 'signal/noise ratio'. We shall use this concept to find out what type of signal is likely to be transmitted along the channels of the world lines that connect twins together, so let us clarify its meaning. The aerial and the receiving equipment of a radio picks up a great deal of information. It is the resonant tuning that filters out most of the unwanted information, but even in the very narrow band of wavelengths associated with a given radio station there will be extra noise coming from a variety of sources, natural and artificial. This noise is incoherent, in that there is no definite phase relationship between the signals arriving at different times, unlike the signal from the radio station, which is coherent. Normally this noise will take the form of a faint hiss on the speaker. However, if the signal coming from the station is strong, this hiss will be swamped by the signal and we say that the signal/noise ratio is large. If they are of equal amplitude, then the hissing will sometimes make the signal indistinct, and if it is greater than the signal it will swamp it.

There are two sources of noise which affect the world-line communication channel. The first is the mass of strong signal information coming into the brain of each twin via its ordinary sense organs. The second is all the encounters the twins have had with other people since birth. These sources of noise will, for the most part, swamp the signals coming along the world-line channel. This is a good defence mechanism for both twins. It means that they can lead reasonably separate lives. However, it may well be that large departures from the status quo may generate strong signals which can overcome the noise in the channel. How this could happen is illustrated in the next section, which starts with analogies.

Emotional Tyre Noise

First, when a car is riding along a reasonably straight road at a constant speed, there is usually only a slight hum of noise as the tyres move over the road surface. However, tyre noise is very noticeable when the brakes are applied abruptly, or in taking a corner at high speed or when accelerating violently. There is an equivalent to this in physics. When a charged particle is moving through space at a constant speed, without any change of direction, it radiates no electromagnetic radiation. When the particle changes speed or direction for any reason, it begins to radiate. This type of radiation is called bremsstrahlung – from the German *bremsen*, to brake, and *Strahlung*, meaning radiation. I am proposing that there exists a kind of 'emotional bremsstrahlung', which can send strong signals along the world-line channel of communication between twins.

Such emotional bremsstrahlung can be generated during moments of intense physical and emotional pain, such as those which we all experience when we suffer physical injury or an emotional trauma.

This will explain why twins can suffer synchronized emotional pain, as when a relative dies, or why one twin can suffer pain when the other twin is injured. Since death is the ultimate emotional trauma, this can also explain why there have been cases of twins dying together. This concept also explains why it has been difficult to reproduce the infrequent telepathic communication between twins in controlled laboratory situations.

Still to be explained however are cases in which twins who have been separated at birth have been given very similar names. I am proposing that when they are young, they have had fewer other interactions with people, so their telepathic world-line channel is still relatively clear, and messages can be passed along it. Such children can then act, quite unconsciously, as telepathic telephones for the, again unconscious, transmission of ideas from the one group of adopted or foster parents to the other. In other words this provides us with an example of 'naming resonance'.

In this chapter we have looked at some strange forms of communication between twins, identical and non-identical. We have briefly mentioned some of the ideas which have been proposed to explain this type of communication. We have seen that some instances may be understood in terms of biomagnetic tidal resonance, but that this theory could not cope with all the examples. These exceptions can, however, be explained if there exist relatively clear world-line-web channels of communication between twins. In the next chapter we apply these ideas to phenomena such as telepathy, clairvoyance, retrocognition and ghosts.

10 | From Telepathy to Apparitions

Lives of great men all remind us
We can make our lives sublime,
And, departing, leave behind us
Footprints on the sands of time.
            H. W. Longfellow

We are all sublime, because we all leave our footprints on the sands of time. As we move about, as we create our personalities within the constraints imposed on us by our genetic inheritance, as we establish our own patterns of behaviour and we turn some of these patterns into habits, so we are leaving our footprints on the sands of time.

In the last few chapters we have discussed the theory that charged particles trail braided fibre bundles of electrified plasma space along as they move about and interact with each other. Thus they become the shuttles that have woven a web of electrified world lines which can push all particles around, giving rise to the quantum noise of the universe. These shuttles not only wove the past, they are also weaving the present and they will weave the future. This theory leads to the inevitable consequence that the present is merely the moving fringe on an evolving space-time tapestry, which had its origin in the Big Bang, and the loom of which was the evolution of all the matter in the universe right up to the present time. The various stages of this evolution, including the evolution of life on Earth, are thus stratified in this space-time tapestry. This world view enables one to unify quantum mechanics with relativity, but it also opens up the possibility of explaining some phenomena that have been labelled, in the past, as paranormal phenomena.

Telepathy

Telepathy has already been mentioned in the case of identical twins, but here we will consider the matter in more detail, with particular emphasis on the role of the space-time web for this type of communication. As pointed out by Brian Inglis in his book *The Paranormal:*

An Encyclopedia of Psychic Phenomena, one of the first presentations on the subject at a scientific meeting was made by William Barrett, Professor of Physics at the Royal College of Science in Dublin, during the 1876 annual meeting of the British Association for the Advancement of Science. Human nature being what it is, some members of this association were disgusted that such a subject should be aired at one of its meetings. Barrett's paper was based on observations he had made during an experiment on mesmerism which was carried out by a friend. During one of these experiments a child was being tested, and Barrett noticed that this child could 'taste' and 'feel' what the mesmerist was tasting and feeling. He referred to this as a 'community of sensation', and added that 'ideas or emotions occurring in the operator appeared to be reproduced in the subject without the intervention of any sign, or visible or audible communication'.

The term telepathy was actually introduced by Frederic Myers, who wished to distinguish the scientific study of the subject from the music-hall acts of 'thought reading', which were merely tricks. He defined telepathy as 'the communication of impressions of any kind from one mind to another independently of the recognized channels of the senses'.

All thought processes are accompanied by chemical and electrical changes in the brain, and so they involve temporal changes in the positions and patterns of subatomic particles. Since the world-line web threads its way through all the matter in the universe, it will pick up the vibrations resulting from these changes. It is thus likely that the evolving thought patterns of one person can be picked up by another person, in much the same way as a radio receiver can, because of resonance, be tuned to a specific radio station, but in this case the medium will be the world-line web, and not electromagnetic vibrations that occur in the spaces between the web. However, the effect will be stronger if the world lines of the two people concerned have crossed or, still better, run very closely together in the past. Thus telepathic communication is likely, as we have already seen, to be stronger with identical twins, but it is also likely to be strong in families, and theoretically possible between any two people, provided they become resonantly 'tuned' to each other.

Evidence in support of the contention that telepathic communication is likely to be strong between members of families, comes from the following story recounted by Brian Inglis, about Gilbert Murray, a highly regarded academic figure of his time, who was President of the Society for Psychical Research in 1915: 'Murray would go out of the room while members of his family and guests decided on a subject; it would be written down; and he would be called back and asked to guess it.' In one of the examples quoted by Inglis the subject chosen was the sinking of the *Lusitania*. Murray said, 'I've got this violently. I've got an awful impression of naval disaster. I should think it was the torpedoing of the *Lusitania*.'

Clairvoyance, Clairaudience and Clairvoyant Reality

Stuart Holroyd, in *The Arkana Dictionary of New Perspectives*, defines clairvoyance as 'the ability to receive extrasensory knowledge of a thing or event that is not known to any other human being at the time'. This too can be understood in terms of the world-line-web model of extrasensory reality. The basic subatomic particles are localizations of energy within the world-line web. Atoms are a particular form of dance of these subatomic particles within the web, and thus set up spatial and temporal vibration patterns of the web. Molecules are colonies of atoms, each performing a different type of dance in space-time. Thus atoms and molecules all impose different sets of vibrating patterns on the world-line web. Objects are much larger colonies of atoms and molecules, which also impose their own signature tunes and patterns on the web of world lines. Events usually involve changes in the positions of objects, and thus they are temporal patterns, of limited duration, in the positions of objects. Some people, who we classify as clairvoyants, are able to pick up these patterns, via resonance, in much the same way as a dowser can detect changes in the fluctuations of the geomagnetic field associated with the flow of water or with special types of rock formation. Just as dowsers have had to develop their ability to detect and identify these changes, so clairvoyants have had to discover and develop their abilities.

Clairaudience is the term used to describe voices, or sounds, heard in the inner ear as if they were real. The sounds from the human voice, the music coming from an orchestra and the rustle of leaves in the wind all have their distinctive signatures of vibration. Normally these sounds are transmitted by molecules of air which are periodically changing their spatial relationship to each other. These molecules consist of atoms which are made from subatomic particles which are riding the tides of the world-line web, and they in turn are setting up their own patterns of vibrations on the web, so it is possible to transmit the 'sound' via the world-line web, through resonance. This is not, in some ways, dissimilar to modulating radio waves by sound waves at a radio station, which are then transmitted in such a way that they can be picked up by a receiver tuned to that station, and decoded into sound waves once again.

The idea that there are two distinct orders of reality has been proposed by Lawrence LeShan. Besides the 'sensory reality', with which we are all familiar, there exists, LeShan argues, another reality which he labels 'clairvoyant reality'. According to LeShan, paranormal faculties develop when people move out of their normal sensory mode into a mode in which they can perceive clairvoyant reality. He argues that the difference between the two orders is mainly a difference of thought and attitude. The majority of us spend most of our time on the level of sensory reality, basing our world view on the information which we receive from our senses. A very clear and concise statement of the views of LeShan is given by Stuart Holroyd: 'We see people and things as separate entities, and we consider the most important things about them to be the properties that make them individual. From the other point of view . . . the important thing about an individual is his or her relation to the rest of the universe. All beings – and even inanimate things like rock, water and earth – are seen as parts of a whole.'

In support of his views, LeShan quotes from the writings of several modern physicists, and in particular he gives the following quote from J. Robert Oppenheimer, the well-known atomic physicist and father of the atom bomb: 'These two ways of thinking, the way of time and history and the way of eternity and timelessness, are both parts of man's efforts to comprehend the world in which he lives. Neither is comprehended in the other nor reducible to it. They are, as we have learned to say in physics, complementary views, each supplementing the other, neither telling the whole story.'

Retrocognition and Ghosts

Brian Inglis discusses some examples of retrocognition in his book. In particular he mentions the book *An Adventure*, written in 1911, by the Oxford dons Annie Moberly and Eleanor Jourdain (who used the pseudonyms of Miss Morison and Miss Lamont). This book describes how, when they visited Versailles, they saw people, and the buildings and grounds, as they were in the days of Louis XVI and Marie Antoinette. In his book *Hauntings and Apparitions* Andrew MacKenzie produced some impressive confirmation for the reality of the experience of these dons. Many people have had similar experiences, although they have not been recorded in as much detail as this one.

Such retrocognitive experiences are often associated with a particular place, so they are quite often referred to as '*déjà vu*' experiences, when people feel that they 'have been here before'. Some of these experiences can quite naturally be understood in terms of the world-line-web model of extrasensory reality. The world lines passing through a particular place at a particular time are continuous with the world lines that passed through that place at an earlier time. This is particularly true if physical relics of the earlier time are still preserved at the later date. The retrocognition is also likely to be stronger if some ancestor of the person having such an experience in the present (along a direct genetic line) visited the place in the past. There is then a clearer world-line channel linking the present and past.

Ghosts and Apparitions

The same type of reasoning can be applied to the seeing of ghosts. A person of firm and strong habits who had lived at the same place for a very long time would leave a strong 'imprint' on the world lines passing through that place. The apparition is very often described as being unclear or fuzzy. The quality of the image can be attributed to the fact that the world lines have had several other encounters if the person to whom the ghost 'belongs' died a long time ago, in which case the space-time channel will be more 'noisy'. The 'noise' in the channel becomes less important if there is fine resonant tuning between the person receiving the image and the ghost transmitting it. Once again, it may be possible for anyone to tune in to this image, via resonances with the space-time web of memory, but the image is likely to be stronger if the viewer is a direct descendant of the dead person, or if they have been close friends, in which case the world lines would have interacted frequently in the past.

Let us look at some specific examples in order to illustrate these concepts. First of all we should make it clear that most researchers into the field of paranormal phenomena no longer use the word 'ghost', first because of its vagueness and second because of its popular connotations. It is now more acceptable, in paranormal research, to talk about apparitions, and these are now put into three different categories: those associated with people still living, those of people who are dying and those of the dead.

Doppelgängers

Doppelgänger is the term sometimes applied to any apparition of a living person, but it is more frequently applied in the case of a persistent double. Several such cases have been reported.

A story is related about the German poet, scholar and statesman, Johann Wolfgang von Goethe. The poet was, on one occasion, walking back to his home with a friend, when he stopped very suddenly, and said, 'If I weren't sure that my friend Frederick was at this moment in Frankfurt, I'd swear it was he!' Apparently this puzzled the friend he was walking with, because he had seen no one. Goethe thought that he must have been hallucinating, and became worried, thinking that it might indicate that Frederick had just died. To his great relief, when he got home he found his friend waiting for him. While waiting for the return of Goethe, Frederick had fallen asleep in an armchair in Goethe's house, and had dreamed that he had gone out to meet his friend.

Another case that is of interest, because it involves a corroborating witness, is that related by S. R. Wilmot. He was returning from America in a ship, *The City of Limerick*, when they ran into a fierce storm, and for eight days he got very little sleep. When the storm subsided, he had his first good sleep, and dreamed that his wife came into the cabin in her nightdress, and hesitated, seeing he was not alone, but nevertheless 'stooped and kissed me, and after having caressed me a few moments she quietly withdrew'. On waking up he found his cabin mate, W. J. Tait, looking at him in a fixed manner. Tait then said, 'You are a lucky fellow to have a lady come to visit you like that!' On his return home, the first thing his wife told him was that she had deliberately visualized that she was visiting him, at the time he had the dream, because she had heard of the storms that were raging in the Atlantic.

Both the above cases can be seen as telepathic thought transference, through resonance, via the world-line web. In the latter case, the third participant, W. J. Tait, could have been picking up the associated pattern of world-line-web vibrations because of his close proximity to one member of a pair who had world lines that had run intimately together with those of the other in the past. In either case, it is difficult to tell how much was filled in by the brain after the initial contact was made via the world-line-web channel of communication. This type of information transference can be compared to the transmission of a television picture from the television station to a receiver tuned to that station. The picture is taken at the studio in the form of variations of light, colour and sound, but these are then converted, by the transmission equipment, into variations in amplitude and time of the basic electromagnetic waves which are used to broadcast the picture. At the tuned receiver the information is then reassembled to form a recognizable picture, accompanied by coherent sound. Television receivers act as secondary relay television transmitters, or, alternatively, we can say that they scatter the incoming information. It is this scattered information that is picked up by the television detector vans that search out people who have not paid for a television licence. We can say that Tait was the 'television detector van' picking up scattered signals from Wilmot's world-line-web 'television set'.

One of the best-known instances of the persistent appearance of the double of a person, is that involving Emelie Sagee, who was a teacher at a school for young ladies in Livonia. In the mid-1840s, her pupils frequently reported seeing her double in the school grounds while she was still inside the classroom. On occasions her double behaved as if it was imitating what she was doing, and on other occasions her double was doing something different. Stories of her 'bilocation' soon spread, but because she was a good teacher, the directors of the school were reluctant to dismiss her, until some of the parents withdrew their daughters from the school as a result of these stories. Apparently she told the children that she had been dismissed from other schools for the same reason. In this particular case it is possible to see those instances when the double was acting differently to Emelie herself as being examples of retrocognition, in which the viewers were seeing earlier sections of the world-line tapestry associated with this woman's life. Some of those instances in which the *doppelgänger* was mimicking her movements could also be seen as a 'bilocated' resonance effect, in which her present movements were resonating with earlier similar movements along her world lines, but some of them might have been due to resonance scattering off someone else in the school with whom she had been closely associated. We do not know why this happened so strongly in this unusual case. Was the young lady undergoing a continuing emotional identity crisis which caused her to emit the type of emotional bremsstrahlung we mentioned in the previous chapter? Since we do not have enough information on her mental and emotional state, and since we do not have other cases with which to compare her, we cannot give any convincing answers to these questions.

Apparitions of the Dying

There have been several accounts of apparitions of people who are dying appearing to relatives and friends. Sometimes the visual apparition is silent, but there have been instances in which the vision was accompanied by sound. Frederic Myers, one of the founders of the Society for Psychical Research, was very impressed by a story concerning a Fellow of the Royal Society, the Canadian biologist and psychologist G. J. Romanes. Although this story had no attestation, what impressed Myers was that Romanes was part of the rationalist camp that included Tyndall, Huxley and Darwin. In a letter to Myers, Romanes described how he saw his bedroom door open, and a shrouded figure enter the room and move towards the foot of his bed. 'Then with its two hands it suddenly parted the shroud over the face, revealing between its two hands the face of my sister.' At this time Romanes knew that his sister was ill, but was under the impression that it was not a serious illness, until seeing this apparition. The following day he called Sir William Jenner, her physician, who told him that his sister had only a few days to live. This did indeed turn out to be the case.

Another story concerns the Scots poet William Drummond. Ben Jonson was staying with Drummond at the time of the Great Plague. Drummond kept a record of their conversations which took place at this time, and relates that one day Jonson 'saw' his eldest child, then living in London, 'with the mark of a bloody cross on his forehead, as if it had been cut with a sword'. Not long after this Jonson received a letter to say the boy had died of the plague.

One case, often referred to, is that relating to the death of David McConnel, an officer in the Royal Flying Corps. The story is told in a letter which James Larkin, a fellow officer, wrote to David's father. According to Larkin, he was sitting in his room when the door opened 'with the usual noise and clatter which David always made. I heard his "Hello, boy", and turned around in my chair and saw him standing in the doorway, dressed in his flying clothes.' After exchanging a few words with Larkin, 'he said, "Well, cheerio!", closed the door noisily and went out'. Later on Larkin found out that very close to this time David had been killed in an air crash.

Apparitions of the dying are consistent with the proposal, made in the last chapter, that people undergoing severe physical or emotional pain can emit emotional bremsstrahlung via the world-line web to people who have been close to them in the past. Death may be, to many people, the ultimate in pain, emotional or physical.

Hauntings

Andrew Lang was in 1911 President of the Society for Psychical Research. Besides being a novelist, an historian and an anthropologist, he was an expert on folk customs and folklore. He held that '. . . the essential characteristic of a true haunt is that it is related to place'. One of the committees of the Society for Psychical Research, founded in 1882, was charged with the task of investigating reports, 'resting on strong testimony', regarding disturbances in houses reputed to be haunted. One of the most remarkable stories collected by this committee, concerns 'the tall woman in black'.

Apparently this woman walked about the home of the Despard family in Cheltenham, 'as if resident' there. On several occasions she was mistaken for a guest by visitors who were unaware that the house was haunted. On different occasions she was heard by more than twenty people, and seen, at various times, by seventeen people. The members of the committee were very impressed by the consistency of the accounts of the physical appearance of the apparition. Most people also agreed that she held a handkerchief to the lower part of her face. On a few occasions she was seen to come into a room and stay for a while, and when she left the room, she would on some occasions be seen independently by two people. On several different occasions the family heard sounds coming from parts of the house which were known to be empty. These sounds took the form of the turning of door handles, bumps against doors, and the sound of footsteps on the second-floor landing.

One member of the family, Rosian Despard, conducted her own research on the apparition. When she heard the tall lady descending the stairs she fastened fine string across the stairs, at varying heights, and then reported that she saw the tall lady 'pass through the cords, leaving them intact'. She also tried to touch the apparition on several occasions, but never succeeded in doing so.

The novelist L. A. G. Strong recounts a story about an apparition who haunted the masters' residence at the Oxford preparatory school where Strong was a teacher at the time. On one occasion he saw a man with a brown moustache, with some musical scores under his arm, enter a room then occupied by one of the other masters, W. S. Case. Since Case, who was a friend of Strong, also had a moustache and sometimes carried music about with him, it was very natural for Strong to assume it was Case. However, when Strong went over to Case's room, Case was not there. When Case arrived Strong told him the story, to which Case replied, 'Oh, that was Winsford Allington. He was killed in 1917. He played the organ here before me. This was his room.'

Harold Owen, brother of the poet Wilfred Owen, tells a story about the death of his brother. This case is unusual in that the apparition of Wilfred Owen appeared to Harold in his cabin on board a Royal Naval cruiser on which Harold was an officer. The cruiser was just leaving the Cameroons, which was a place never visited by Wilfred in his lifetime. Soon after seeing the apparition Harold was to learn that Wilfred had been killed in action on the Western Front, a few days before the armistice.

A rather unusual case comes to us from the files of the parapsychology laboratory of Duke University in Durham, North Carolina. In this case a man who had bought a second-hand motor bike was repairing the bike in the yard of his house, being watched by his wife. She saw a young man enter the yard, and then proceed to take a keen interest in the work her husband was doing. When she asked her husband to introduce her to the man, he disappeared. It turned out that her husband had not seen the man, but she was able to give a clear description of him. On making some inquiries, the couple found out that a man of that description had owned the bike, and had been killed on it two years before he was seen as an apparition by the wife. Since he must have ridden the bike for some time, his world lines would have run in parallel with those of the bike. The woman could have been picking up a fossilized past image of the young man via the world lines that terminated in the present position of the motor bike.

An Alternative Theory of Ghosts

Cyril Smith and Simon Best, in their book *Electromagnetic Man*, put forward an alternative theory for ghosts. They say:

At death, the whole entity of a person's 'acquired' information field must become separated from the body which is about to commence decay, if it is to retain any objective existence in the material world ... There is the possibility that information could be 'written' into environmental water, such as that retained in the stone or brick of a building. The necrotic radiation, if this is indeed an electromagnetic field phenomenon, could be the origin of such memories in locations for events which happen there. The possibility of 'fixing' a dowsable 'charge' into stones by cremation supports this view. Effects corresponding to the frequencies of electromagnetic fields can be precisely retained by water for extended periods. If this is the case, then a reacting hypersensitive allergic subject should be able to 'read out' this information at a later time, just as if they were accessing a magnetic tape or a hologram ... This information might also be holographic in nature and be interpreted as an actual presence at that point in space and time, that is the person might 'see a ghost'.

I have certain reservations about the explanation given by Smith and Best. If water can retain a memory of certain electromagnetic frequencies for extended periods, environmental water is very subject to change, by evaporation and by convection, so it is extremely difficult to see how it can retain memories that could give rise to ghostly apparitions for very long periods of time. In order to make a hologram one needs the coherent light that you get from a laser. Although Smith and Best have argued for coherent electromagnetic oscillations within biological systems, it is also difficult to see how such coherency can be maintained over a fairly large frequency range for long enough for the memory to be stored in environmental water.

According to the theory of the world-line-web memory, the past is permanently 'fossilized' in space and time, and so one can have access to events that happened a long time ago. However, for the most part the signals coming from the past will be of the same order as the quantum noise within the world-line web; in other words, the signal/noise ratio will be very nearly equal to one another, which implies that the signal is only as strong as the noise. If there is some resonance between the present receiver and the transmitter in the past, then this will increase the amplitude of the signal compared to that of the noise. The signal is even stronger if there are relatively clear world-line channels between transmitter and receiver. Earlier on we saw that the signals also tend to be swamped by information which is received from the sense organs of our normal five senses. This source of 'sensory noise' can also tend to swamp the 'paranormal signals' coming from other locations in space and time. This source of noise is likely to be reduced if the brain of the receiver or the transmitter is in a resting state. The strength of the signal can be considerably increased, if a living transmitter is emitting emotional bremsstrahlung because of some traumatic experience, like intense physical or mental pain. Thus the world-line-web model of quantum reality is able to explain some of the examples of so-called paranormal experience.

Morphic Resonance, Astrology and
     Precognition

> From Harmony, from heavenly Harmony
>   This universal Frame began:
>   From Harmony to Harmony
> Through all the compass of the notes it ran,
> The diapason closing full in Man.
>
> John Dryden, 'Song for St Cecilia's Day', 1687

We have not yet dealt with the subject of precognition. Since the
whole concept of precognition seems to imply that the future has its
roots in the present, it is necessary to discuss its relationship with
other disciplines that claim to be able to predict the future. In
particular we have to consider its relationship to astrology, because
this subject has always been, at least to some extent, concerned with
forecasting the future. We have also considered the relationship
between astrology and other subjects that could be relevant to a
foreknowledge of future events. Some recent writers on astrology
have considered the concepts of morphic resonance, the soul and
reincarnation to be important to an understanding of astrological
causation, so we will also briefly consider these views. We will
consider a few examples of precognition, and then we will see if they
can be understood in terms of the hypotheses made in this and
previous chapters.

Morphogenetic Fields, Morphic Resonance and Astrology

Sheldrake's ideas have also recently been discussed in connection
with astrology. In his book *The Message of Astrology*, Peter Roberts
has this to say:

As so often happens, proposals for radically new models are greeted
sceptically by the orthodox establishment and Sheldrake is receiving
short shrift. However, if enough favourable evidence accumulates, Sheldrake's theory may become the new orthodoxy. It seems likely that models
which could explain the heterogeneous collection of evidence for astro-

logical effects will need to go beyond the boundaries of contemporary science.

In an article entitled 'A New Hypothesis to Explain Astrology', which appeared in the *Astrological Journal* in 1988, Alan Jewsbury has this to say about the fields proposed by Sheldrake:

These fields are of enormous significance for astrology. Here at last is a possible explanation of . . . how the interaction of controlling fields at birth could build into the personal field a pattern that is influenced or mirrored by the planetary positions at the time.

Jewsbury also quotes Liz Greene as saying:

But we might add something more creative to the archetypal pattern before it passes down to our children. I think we call that evolution.

Then he adds his own assessment of this statement:

This is a statement full of insight based on deep astrological experience, although it is complete nonsense based on current ideas of genetics. Yet it follows exactly from Sheldrake's ideas. Once you understand and accept the possibility of morphic resonance you begin to appreciate the implications and all sorts of unexplained experiences start to drop into place.

Further along in his article Jewsbury also briefly mentions a review, by Robert Hand, of theories of astrological influence:

The one he [Robert Hand] favours is the Clock Theory, which is the most prevalent. It is the mystical one which believes that Man and Nature are one whole, so that the astrological clock can speak a cosmic language. But it is, he says, 'a somewhat foggy metaphor' that 'does not allow us to relax in the belief that we know something'. Now the fog is lifting. Sheldrake's hypothesis is like the strong sunlight breaking through to disperse the fog and will give a well-founded theoretical framework on which to work.

The possibility of a relationship between my theory of astrology, the work of Dennis Elwell, described in his book *Cosmic Loom*, and the work of Sheldrake, is also discussed by Daniele Patton in an article entitled 'Are We Really Back to Aquinas?', which appeared in the *Astrological Journal* in 1989. In the abstract of her article, Patton has this to say:

The Saturn/Uranus 1988 planetary mood, upsetting all forms of 'establishment' with radical departures, coincided with the publication of two books giving new theories explaining the astrological phenomenon: *Cosmic Loom: The New Science of Astrology* by Dennis Elwell, and *Astrology: The Evidence of Science* by Percy Seymour. This article will attempt to show that a third book, *The Presence of the Past* by Rupert Sheldrake, puts forward a scientific theory supporting both divergent theories, and offers a conception of the universe which can accommodate both astrologers and scientists . . .

Patton ends her article with these words:

Should this theory [Sheldrake] ever become mainstream, it could open the door to astrology being scientifically accepted as well as giving weight to Dr Seymour's 'magnetic midwifery of the planets' theory. It could also, in the same process, shake astrology's own conceptions to its very roots.

Dennis Elwell stated, without any convincing supporting argument, that Bell's theorem provided support for astrology. I have briefly discussed the difficulties of using Bell's work and quantum mechanics as a basis for astrological phenomena in my book *Astrology: The Evidence of Science*. In the next section I just want to comment briefly on the views of Jewsbury and Patton.

Although astrologers have considered Sheldrake's hypothesis to be an astrological breakthrough, they have not really specified, in any depth, why they believe this to be the case, except in the very general terms quoted above. In the absence of such clarification, these suggestions cannot be processed to the stage of a scientific theory which can be tested by the normal methods of science.

The Scientific Status of Magneto-astrology and Sheldrake's Theory

The theory of magneto-astrology, discussed in detail in my earlier book and more briefly in Chapter 7 of this book, is able to account for the only convincing scientific evidence in favour of astrology in terms of the known physical entities, like the magnetic field of the Sun, the solar wind, lunar magnetic tides in the upper atmosphere, the possibility of resonant tidal coupling between the planets and magnetic activity on the Sun, and the vast and growing evidence of the biological effects of changes in the geomagnetic field. Thus it uses the current scientific framework and extends this, without invoking any new fields, by proposing that the known fields can interact, through resonance, in ways that can explain the evidence which supports a close coupling between the dynamics of the solar system and life on our Earth. The theory has also been formulated in mathematical terms. All this means that it is already couched in terms of mainstream science, and the fact that it is not generally accepted by the scientific community does not alter this. The fact that there is already some evidence in favour of the theory and the fact that it needs to be tested further, are features shared by all other theories. In other words, all scientific theories start as attempts to explain some observations or experiments, but they all go beyond what is already known, and thus they have to be tested in those areas that have not yet yielded information. It should also be understood that it is impossible, in principle, to conceive of all the many circumstances to which the theory might be applicable, so the process of testing is an ongoing scientific enterprise. However, if this testing yields a set of observations that is in conflict with the theory, and it proves impossible to incorporate the new information into the theory as it stands, then the theory either has to be modified or rejected. It should also be pointed out that although it is possible to disprove a scientific theory, it is impossible to prove one conclusively. All that can be said of any theory, no matter how many people believe it to be beyond all reasonable doubt, is that it is consistent with the data available at a given stage in the ongoing process of scientific research.

This point is well made by Karl Popper in *The Logic of Scientific Discovery*: 'The game of science is, in principle, without end. He who decides one day that scientific statements do not call for any further test, and that they can be regarded as finally verified, retires from the game.'

Some science writers and a few scientists, none of them with specialist knowledge in the fields appropriate to the theory of magneto-astrology, have steadfastly refused to consider the evidence on which the theory rests, not because it is suspect in any way, but because it conflicts with their own preconceived ideas. This is a totally unscientific response. They have also refused to consider the mathematical aspects of resonance as applied to magneto-astrology, once again not because it is suspect, but because it offends their own 'common-sense' view of the world. The history of science has shown us, time and again, that our common-sense point of view very often does not provide substantial clues to the way the universe works. Progress is made in science when we realize the limitations of common sense. The arguments put forward by science writers and scientists against the theory cannot be properly described as scientific arguments. They are merely rationalizations of their own prejudices, and are only accepted as 'scientific' by those other scientists who wish to protect and reinforce their own prejudices. These are pseudo-scientific ploys used by some supporters of orthodox science, in their attempts to preserve the status quo and to maintain the intellectually dishonest pretence that all is well with present-day science, and that most of the major problems of science either are, or soon will be, solved.

Sheldrake has a completely different approach. Despite the support his theory has received from some science writers and a few scientists, it has stepped completely outside the realms of modern science. This in itself does not mean that it should be rejected, since all new ideas, as we have already seen, start by stepping outside the current framework. However, all theories of physics that involve fields are accompanied by a set of field equations, and these help us, in principle, to work out the consequences of the theory in precise mathematical terms although in many important cases we are still unable to carry out the actual calculations. Sheldrake has not provided us with such a set of equations. Orthodox genetics has been formulated in precise mathematical terms and mathematical models of evolution, which utilize this formulation, have been investigated. Sheldrake has not provided us with a mathematical formulation of his concept of morphic resonance. I believe Sheldrake was aware of these difficulties, although some of his more vocal science-writer supporters were not, and this is why he labelled it a hypothesis rather than a theory. My own work on the concept of the world-line web started as an attempt to overcome the problem of reconciling relativity and quantum mechanics, but it also provides a more carefully formulated basis for Sheldrake's morphogenetic fields. The theory of magneto-astrology makes it unnecessary to involve the world-line-web concept, or Sheldrake's ideas, in explanations of the scientific evidence for some astrological phenomena. However, I do believe that the world-line-web memory sheds some light on the evolution of biological clocks, and it can also be used to understand the links between astrology and premonitions. These are topics that will be discussed in the following section.

Astrology, the Soul and Reincarnation

Two recent books have proposed theories of astrology which involve non-physical or spiritual concepts. The first is *The Message of Astrology* by Peter Roberts, in which he comments on the magnetic theory of astrology:

Seymour is still developing his theory ... However, it does seem, even at this stage, that there is good reason to believe that the Seymour theory contains elements of the truth. Whether it will ultimately explain all of the evidence seems unlikely, but Seymour has said that even if there are paranormal links involved in astrology, his mission is to establish how much of it can be explained on straightforward scientific principles.

At one point in his book he has this to say:

There is an entity which is separate from the physical body, both preexisting it and surviving it. The entity attempts to choose an appropriate time to be born – but it can be thwarted by external interference ...

Charles Harvey has reviewed Roberts's book in a recent issue of the *Astrological Journal*, where he comments:

Roberts's message is that his detailed analyses of the now hard evidence for astrological effects, and in particular the planetary effects of the Gauquelins, and his considerations of all the various astrological models and hypotheses from the synchronistic to the electromagnetic, now compel us to bring the Soul back into our model of man. It is his conclusion that without such an entity no explanation of the known facts seems to be possible ...

Penny Thornton in her book *The Forces of Destiny: Reincarnation, Karma and Astrology* has a similar point of view:

Dr Seymour has provided a very workable model for the way in which planets forge a link with human destiny. However, to my mind there is a fatal flaw in his proposal that the tuning of the nervous system depends on the genetically inherited personality of the individual. I have already presented an alternative psychological and mystical view of the role of the personality and the way supersensible forces, including planetary and zodiacal, fashion the psychic structure of the individual prior to the physical. Thus, as I would see it, the planetary patterns from the moment of conception synchronize with the individual, and throughout gestation resonate with his psychic and physical being, so that his birth is not only triggered by the appropriate planetary 'chords', but he enters the world at a time that astrologically reflects precisely who he is – his fate, his destiny, his karma.

I have some sympathy with these points of view, but I would not see it as necessary to invoke the soul or similar spiritual concepts to explain the most convincing evidence in favour of astrology. I do think that the world-line web, with its collective memory, may well possess some of the qualities required by Roberts and Thornton, and it might play some part in astrology, but I would place this second to the role of the geomagnetic field, its cosmically linked fluctuations and the biological effects of these on the personality, both before and after birth.

The World-line Web and the Origin of Biological Clocks

When studying for an examination, or learning lines for a play, we all know that we need to have the material fresh in our minds. Detectives interviewing people after an accident, or after a crime has been committed, know that it is important to carry out the interview shortly after the incident, when the memory is still clear and few other things have happened that might make it less clear. We have already seen that if two systems have world lines that have crossed in the past, and little has happened since, then there will be a fairly clear channel in the world-line memory, which is a means of communication between the systems. This is one way in which the world-line memory resembles ordinary human memory. There is, however, another way in which the two types of memory resemble each other. We can reinforce our memories by repetition. Lines of poetry, tunes or mathematical formulae can be memorized in this way. Similarly the world-line memory can be strengthened by repetition, and this is a way in which cosmic, planetary, geophysical and biological cycles can become recurring themes of the world-line web.

The evolutionary tuning of biological clocks via the genes may well be assisted by the vibrations of the world-line web. We have already seen that systems that interacted in the past, either directly, or via some mediating field or fields, will have had some effect on each other's world lines, and this could have been fossilized in the memory of the world-line web. We have seen that it is likely that the memory of the world-line web was strengthened by repetition, and so cyclic patterns would be stronger than infrequent or non-periodic events. Living organisms developed biological clocks to give them evolutionary advantages by adapting to the useful regularities of their environment. Thus some species would survive and strengthen their own world-line memories if they had internal biological clocks whose world lines ran parallel to those of certain cosmically linked geophysical cycles. They could tune in to the past of their own species via the chain of gene telephone exchanges which gives them a clear channel to past events.

The Origins of Astrology and Precognition

The ability of a few people to anticipate some events, and some of the future reactions of people known to them, is very closely linked, I believe, to the origins of astrology. The theory of magneto-astrology proposes, as we have already seen, that the positions and movements of the planets are the controlling factors in the solar cycle, and it is well known that this cycle influences the geomagnetic field via the solar wind. This in turn interferes with the compass needle, and there is evidence that it can also influence the internal 'magnetic compasses' of animals and humans. There is also evidence that the ability to dowse is connected to the detection of specific fluctuations of the geomagnetic field which are linked to the flow of underground water. The early sky watchers might well have discovered that the movements of the Sun, Moon and planets interfered with their ability to find direction and dowse. This seems to be the most straightforward way for our general cosmic awareness to have developed into a more complex and structured body of knowledge.

It is likely that people with different characters 'heard' different magnetic tunes from the celestial spheres, because of genetic differences in the tuning of their nervous-system aerials. Thus, for example, those of a warlike disposition 'heard' martial music, whereas those of a jovial disposition 'heard' the music of Jupiter. Thus the human ability to detect magnetic fields formed a framework into which other changes, such as the meteorological effects of changes in the geomagnetic field, could be fitted. During violent sunspot activity it is not unknown for the northern lights to be seen further south. This too would thus have been associated with those times when ancient man found it difficult to dowse and find direction. I think it is likely that this is how astrology developed, some time before it was more formally systematized by the work of the Babylonians and the Greeks.

The 'music of the spheres' has become fossilized into the memory of the space-time web and also closely woven into those reactions it tended to promote in people and terrestrial events. Those people who are able to get fleeting glimpses of a few events and reactions that still lie in the future are what I would call natural astrologers. They can perhaps pick up the vibrations of the world-line web, and by doing so they can perhaps read the recurring themes in the musical score of the cosmos: by picking up the 'magnetic music of the spheres' being broadcast at a given time, they know how the rest of the human orchestra could be reacting at that time and how they might react in the future. If for example they have been able to identify certain people as 'Venus violinists' or 'Saturn saxophonists' they can perhaps anticipate how such people might react in the future, to a certain part of the music – provided, of course, that these people are listening! This does *not* imply that we are predestined to behave in a certain way, but rather that the cosmos might predispose us to act in one way rather than another.

Evidence for Precognition

Some of the evidence for precognitive experiences is very suspect. This stems from the fact that in many cases, people only recount such experiences once the event has occurred, and then it is difficult to separate the details of the actual experience from those of the supposed premonition. There are, however, some examples that are not open to this criticism. One set of such examples is associated with the sinking of the *Titanic* in April 1912, with the loss of some fifteen hundred lives.

A Mr J. C. Middleton booked a passage on the *Titanic* on 23 March 1912. He had a dream about ten days before the sailing date in which '... I saw her [the *Titanic*] floating on the sea, keel upwards and her passengers and crew swimming around her'. Apparently the dream was repeated on the following night, but he did not cancel his passage until about four days later, when a cable arrived from New York telling him to postpone his sailing for a few days, for business reasons. It was then that he told some friends and members of the family about his dreams. These people were thus aware of his precognitive experience *before* the sailing of the ship. The reports of two people confirming this were published in the *Proceedings of the Society for Psychical Research*.

Professor Ian Stevenson collected a number of phenomena associated with the sinking of the *Titanic* that might be thought of as paranormal, and ten of these, according to Professor A. E. Roy, 'were ostensibly precognitive'. The example quoted above was one of these, but there were others. One of these was quoted by Roy in his book *A Sense of Something Strange*:

Mr V. N. Turvey, a sensitive, predicted on Wednesday, 10 April, that a 'great liner will be lost'. On Saturday, 13 April, he sent this prediction in a letter to Madame I. de Steiger, adding that the liner would be lost in two days. Madame de Steiger received the letter on 15 April a few hours after the *Titanic* sank.

Another possibly precognitive experience, often quoted by writers who discuss the sinking of the *Titanic*, concerns the novel *Futility*, by Morgan Robertson, published in 1898. The book describes the building of a great ocean liner called the *Titan*, which was considered to be unsinkable, and sank after striking an iceberg. There were many striking similarities between the *Titan* and the *Titanic*. Below we list some of those noted by Stevenson, and quoted by Roy. The numbers in the brackets refer to the corresponding data of the *Titanic*:

Number of persons aboard	3,000	(2,207)
Number of lifeboats	24	(20)
Speed at impact with iceberg	25 knots	(23 knots)
Displacement tonnage of the liner	75,000	(66,000)
Length of the liner	800 feet	(882.5 feet)
Number of propellers	3	(3)

Although Professor Stevenson found ten points of correspondence between the real *Titanic* and the fictional *Titan*, which may point to precognition, he nevertheless pointed out that inference, coupled with intelligent guessing, may be able to account for some of the coincidences, or close similarities. He writes:

A writer of the 1890s familiar with man's repeated hubris might reasonably infer that he would overreach himself in the construction of ocean liners which then, with skyscrapers and airplanes, were man's greatest engineering marvels. Granting then a penetrating awareness of man's growing and excessive confidence in marine engineering, a thoughtful person might make additional inferences about the tragedy to come. A large ship would probably have great power and speed; the name *Titan* has connoted power and security for several thousand years: overconfidence would neglect the importance of lifeboats; recklessness would race the ship through the areas of the Atlantic icebergs: these drift south in the spring, making April a likely month for collision.

In summary, I think one might infer that confidence would, for a time, suppress caution in the building and management of ocean liners. Robertson was not the only person to think this.

An alternative point of view of Morgan Robertson's work comes to us from Brian Inglis:

Some of the *Titanic*'s features might have been predicted by a Jules Verne or an H. G. Wells; but there is nothing to show that Robertson had the necessary inside knowledge. In any case, he did not claim to write from inside knowledge, but as a medium. 'He implicitly believed,' a friend wrote, 'that some discarnate soul, some spirit entity with literary ability, denied physical expression, had commandeered his body and brain for the purpose of giving to the world the literary gems which made him famous.'

There was also at least one indication that traditional astrology pointed to such a disaster at sea. It involved the great crusading journalist and editor of the *Pall Mall Gazette*, W. T. Stead, who actually went down with the ship. Stead was known to have consulted two sensitives, on various occasions, concerning future events. On 21 June 1911, Cheiro, a palmist, wrote to Stead, telling him that

. . . from your date of birth in the sign of Cancer, otherwise known as the First House of Water, in my humble opinion, any danger of violent death to you must be by water and nothing else. Very critical and dangerous for you should be April 1912, especially about the middle of the month. So don't travel by water if you can help it. If you do, you will be liable to meet such danger to your life that the very worst may happen. I know I am not wrong about this 'water' danger; I only hope I am, or at least that you won't be travelling somewhere about that time.

One astrologer who firmly believes that astrology can predict events like disasters at sea is Dennis Elwell. On 6 September 1987, he gave a lecture to the Astrological Association's annual conference, which he entitled 'How Far Can the Future be Predicted?' During the lecture he had this to say:

When we ask ourselves by what mechanism disasters like the *Titanic* and the *Herald of Free Enterprise* occur, there is only one conclusion. You can't believe that on that black night in 1912 old Neptune was down there in the Atlantic nudging along the iceberg with his trident! When you read the train of events in disasters of this sort, the things that go wrong simultaneously, you realize that what you have here is a conspiracy of sleepwalkers, people being propelled towards the precipice as if in the grip of some post-hypnotic suggestion. On the *Herald* the crewman who was supposed to shut the doors was literally asleep.

. . . As some of you may know, in February I sent registered letters to two shipping carriers about the likely effects on their operations of the March eclipse. At the very least they were promised disrupted schedules, and at the worst a *Titanic*-like disaster. The tragic capsize of the *Herald of Free Enterprise* came just nine days after P & O wrote to say their procedures could cope with the unexpected.

Predicting Events Involving Human Participation

In an earlier chapter we saw that the theory of biocosmic magneto-tidal resonance does admit the possibility that if the solar system plays 'our tune' on the magnetic field of Earth in later life, it can influence, to some extent, the way we react to information coming to our brains from our other five senses. Since many of the people who will enter certain professions and reach the top of their chosen profession will have similarities in their birth charts, it is quite likely that they will react in similar ways to subsequent positions of Sun, Moon and planets. Thus there may well be patterns in certain events involving decisions by people in command. However, the evidence in this area is, at the moment, very tenuous, so the claim that it is possible to predict the future occurrence of such events is not really justified, although it may well be possible to indicate the likelihood of their occurring. This is a part of astrology that needs much more rigorous research.

Psychic Radar

Some of the instances of precognition cannot be explained in the way described above. One example that presents difficulties to the 'astrological precognition' hypothesis, because of its split-second timing, is related by Arthur Koestler in *The Challenge of Chance*. In this story, a young man who had recently suffered a nervous break-down, threw himself in front of an oncoming tube train. Fortunately the train stopped just in time, and so although the man was injured, he was not killed. The strange twist in this case was that the driver had not applied the brakes. According to Koestler, 'Quite independ-ently, some passenger on the train had pulled down the emergency handle. The Underground authorities had interviewed this passenger after the incident, just in case they had grounds for prosecuting him for pulling it "without reasonable cause".' Such instances can be understood if one postulates that some people are extremely sensitive to the vibrations of the world-line web, in the same way that dowsers are sensitive to changes in the geomagnetic field that are associated with running water, or special types of faults in rocks. It is quite likely that people who are sensitive in this way can 'see' the progress of the world lines of some objects and people through the world-line web, and can then, perhaps unconsciously, act on this information. This use of the paranormal web can be compared to the use of radar by flight controllers at airports to prevent collisions between aircraft landing and taking off, even during foggy conditions. The difference between the two is that in the case of the radar, waves are being transmitted from the ground, but in the case of people using vibra-tions of the world-line web, they are passively picking up changes in the signals being transmitted by other people, and sometimes objects. In the case just described above, the young man must have been going through an emotional crisis and so he could have been emitting emotional bremsstrahlung which would have been increased in fre-quency as the tube train approached him (as a result of the world-line web Doppler effect), and it was perhaps on this information that the passenger who pulled the emergency handle acted.

This line of reasoning can also be applied to another case of precognition, also quoted by Brian Inglis. Lady Craik was just about to cross a street in front of a stationary bus 'when she felt a strong hand on her shoulder which pulled her back sharply'. This action prevented her from being run over by a speeding motor cyclist. 'She turned to thank whoever had saved her, but, to her surprise, there was no one within reach.' The world-line-web waves from the speeding motor cyclist would also have been 'Doppler shifted' because the bike was travelling towards her. Her subconscious mind conveyed the danger 'to the normal consciousness by means of a tactile hallucination'.

In this chapter we have seen how it is possible to extend the world-line-web concept to offer an explanation of some examples of precognitive experiences. To use an analogy, if we are looking at a large rug with a fairly large pattern in it which is incomplete, we can nevertheless use our eyes and our brains to fill in the gaps, or even to extend the pattern to points beyond the stage at which the weaving was stopped. The many cycles of the cosmos, of our Earth and of life on Earth, are in the process of weaving a very complex pattern in the world-line tapestry. Sometimes it is not possible to see the overall design over short periods of time, but if we have the ability to look back over longer periods of time, we begin to 'see' snatches of the grand and intricate design. If we can do this, then it may on occasion be possible to get some foretaste of events that are yet to be.

12 | Extensions in Space and Time

The Moving Finger writes; and, having writ,
Moves on: nor all thy Piety nor Wit
    Shall lure it back to cancel half a Line,
Nor all thy Tears wash out a Word of it.
        Edward Fitzgerald, *The Rubáiyát of Omar Khayyám*

All physical bodies have extensions in space. These we call the fields of these bodies. If these fields change in any way we say that the body is radiating, and in most cases this radiation will move away from the body, with the passage of time, so most bodies will also have extensions in time. For hundreds of years people have believed that all living creatures have extensions in space and time. These concepts have taken various forms, from astral bodies to human auras. In a very real scientific sense, the progress of science and technology has shown us that there is indeed substance to these ideas. In this chapter we will look at the relationship between the spiritual ideas and the scientific reality. We will also extend the ideas developed in previous chapters to try to understand some aspects of homoeopathy, since this subject does seem to imply that some substances have effects that extend in time beyond the physical presence of the particles of which the substance is composed. We will start by discussing auras.

Auras

Auras are bands of coloured lights, something like a human rainbow, which are supposed to surround and radiate from the bodies of plants, animals and humans. It is also believed by some people that the markings and colours of the aura convey information on the physical, emotional, mental and spiritual condition of its possessor. One system of interpretation goes as follows: browns for disease, red for desire and anger, green for intellect, pink for pure love and affection, pale blue and purple for healing power and gold for spirituality. It has long been believed that great spiritual leaders radiate light and in art, gods and holy men are often represented with a halo, or a surrounding aura of light. (An aureole surrounds the whole body, and a nimbus is a halo which surrounds the head.)

Baron von Reichenbach claimed, in the nineteenth century, that he had discovered a type of radiation given off by human beings, animals, plants, magnets and crystals, and that this radiation could be seen by some people who were sensitive to it.

W. J. Kilner tried to devise methods of making the aura visible to ordinary people, because he believed that illness caused changes in the aura, so that if one could 'see' it, then it would be possible to use these methods as a diagnostic tool.

Electromagnetic Auras

All bodies which are above the absolute zero of temperature give off a whole range of electromagnetic wavelengths. As we saw in an earlier chapter, when we discussed black-body radiation, most of the energy given off by a body is radiated close to a specific wavelength, and this varies with temperature. This is why there is such a close relationship between the colour of the radiation emitted by a very hot body and its temperature. Thus the colour of a star can be used to get some idea of its temperature. Very hot stars are bluish white, cooler stars are yellow, or orange, and the coolest stars are a reddish colour. This point is well made in the following quotation from Thomas Hardy's *Far from the Madding Crowd*: 'A difference of colour in the stars – oftener read of than seen in England – was really perceptible here. The sovereign brilliancy of Sirius pierced the eye with a steely glitter, the star called Capella was yellow, Aldebaran and Betelgueux shone with a fiery red.'

Since we are much cooler than stars, we emit most of our radiation in the longer-wavelength, infra-red part of the electromagnetic spectrum. As we also saw in an earlier chapter, snakes can actually detect this type of radiation. Over the years scientists and technologists have developed equipment which can detect the infra-red radiation given off by the human body. This equipment can be used as a tool for diagnosing certain types of breast cancer. This is because a diseased part of the body will cause inflammation in the surrounding tissues, so these will be hotter than the rest of the body and hence will radiate at shorter wavelengths than the surrounding areas.

Electric and Magnetic Auras

All muscular and nervous activity in the bodies of humans and animals is accompanied by electrical activity. However, air is a very poor conductor of electricity, and so this activity can only be detected by placing electrodes in contact with the skin. By placing such electrodes around the skull of a human being it is possible to detect the electric activity of the brain. This too has been developed into a tool for medical diagnosis, because certain types of brain disease are associated with abnormal electrical activity of the brain. By placing electrodes in contact with the chest it is possible to pick up the electrical activity of the human heart, and once again this can be used to diagnose the unusual electricity activity that is associated with certain heart diseases. Sea water is a good conductor of electricity and the electrical activity associated with the muscular movements of a swimmer can be detected by the very sensitive electrical detectors of a shark.

Earlier on we also saw that all electrical changes are accompanied by magnetic fields, and these can also be measured by the most recently developed detectors of magnetic fields, which are extremely sensitive. A great deal of work has already been done on the magnetic activity generated by the heart and brain, and so these detectors are also leading to a better understanding of the functioning of these parts of the body. Thus we see that not only are there parts of the body which respond to external magnetic fields, both naturally occurring and artificially produced, but the body itself has its own fields which can yield some information about its internal state.

Water Memories and Homoeopathy

Smith and Best also use the concept of the ability of water to retain memories of electromagnetic frequencies to propose a physical mechanism for homoeopathic medicine. Homoeopathy was started by Samuel Hahnemann, a German physician. In the process of translating a medical textbook, Hahnemann came across an account of the medicinal properties of the bark of the 'fever tree' of the Peruvian Indians. Its properties became more widely known through Juan Lopez, a Jesuit missionary, who had been cured of malaria by an Indian tribal chief. The wife of the Viceroy of Peru, the Countess of

Chinchon, also used it to treat the disease and it is now called chinchona bark, after the countess.

Hahnemann experimented with the substance on himself, and found that after several days he had developed the symptoms of malaria. He came to the conclusion that a substance that would cure a condition in a sick person would induce the symptoms of the condition in a healthy person. This hypothesis was used as the basis of homoeopathic medicine.

He also experimented with other drugs, including quinine. Since this drug has unpleasant side-effects, Hahnemann set out to determine the minimum dose that would be effective. He then discovered that the smaller the dose, the greater the effective cure. He started with one measure of the drug, and mixed this with nine measures of water or alcohol, shook this violently, and thus produced a medicine with a potency of one in ten. He then used one measure of this liquid and mixed it with nine parts of alcohol or water to produce a potency of one in a hundred. Continuing with this process he found that a medicine with a potency of a million million was still able to give the cure, without the side-effects. This is contrary to the accepted principles of science, since at these dilutions there should, in principle, be no particles of the original substance present. Dr G. O. Barnard, of the National Physical Laboratory, proposed that 'what Hahnemann found quite by accident was a means of separating the structural information content of a chemical from its associated chemical mass'. Barnard developed a theory in which water molecules, when shaken up with a substance dissolved in them, might form into long chains of molecules which have the same shape as the molecules of the dissolved substance, and this spacial message of structure could be passed on from one diluting process to the next. The theory proposed by Smith and Best, summarized in the next section, is a more convincing, detailed and plausible development of this general idea.

Electromagnetic Allergy and Homoeopathy

Dr Smith, the senior author of *Electromagnetic Man*, is a physicist working at the University of Salford. During his research work on the biological effects of electromagnetic fields, he became acquainted with the work of Dr Jean Munro and Dr Bill Rea. These two scientists had shown that the concept of allergy could be extended to include illnesses that were triggered electromagnetically, affecting regulatory systems in the human body in the broadest sense. Working with these people, Dr Smith discovered that the allergic reaction could be neutralized by exposing patients suffering from such illnesses to specific electromagnetic frequencies. They discovered that increasing the frequency produced by an electromagnetic oscillator to which the patient was exposed, produced effects similar to the serial dilution of an allergen.

Further experiments showed that the 'neutralizing effect of this frequency can be transferred to a glass phial of water or saline which is known to be tolerated by the patient, by exposing the phial to a magnetic field at this neutralizing frequency. Water treated in this way appears to be clinically effective for one to two months. This water can be used to prevent or relieve an allergic reaction by just having the patient hold the tube . . .' Smith has proposed a theory for how this might occur, and he has extended this to include how homoeopathic cures might be transmitted via water. In *Electromagnetic Man*, he says:

Watterson has already considered the effects of structure waves in water. In order to account for magnetic effects and a memory for frequency it is desirable to think in terms of a helical structure for water, so that the structure waves would occupy those electromagnetic and acoustic modes of propagation appropriate to a helix. These must be capable of being set up in water by the spectrum of coherent oscillations, which uniquely characterizes the chemical bonds comprising the original tincture molecules; or, in the case of electromagnetic potentization, by the frequencies of the electromagnetic fields applied.

For further details the reader is referred to *Electromagnetic Man*. Here we just wish to comment on the relevance of the world-line-web memory to memories that can be retained by water.

Water Memories and the World-line Web

In an earlier chapter we saw that it was possible to store magnetic memories in solids because the sequencing of the alignments of the magnetic particles can be 'frozen' into the solid and, provided the solid is not heated above its Curie temperature or 'demagnetized' by placing it in a very strong, rapidly fluctuating magnetic field, these memories can be retained indefinitely, because the atoms or molecules of the solid do not change their ordering and orientation with respect to each other. A single bar magnet will with time become demagnetized, because the field of each little magnet will try, because of its direction, to disorientate the alignment of its nearest neighbouring particles. This can be prevented by storing a pair of magnets in a box, aligning them in opposite directions, separating them with a piece of wood and placing two soft iron bars, called keepers, across their ends. The continuous loops of magnetic lines of force will stabilize the magnets.

It is not possible, under normal circumstances, to record information in liquids or gases, because the atoms or molecules move with respect to each other, and so they normally cannot retain any sequencing or ordering for any length of time. We also saw that it is possible to produce some ordering in the ions of the plasma state of matter, because the magnetic field lines within the plasma can, if they are strong enough, help to maintain some degree of ordering within the plasma.

A complex molecule consists of a number of different types of atom arranged in a way unique to that particular chemical. Because of the elaborate recycling of matter that has gone on in the universe, the electrons and protons within such a molecule will, according to the world-line-web model, be trailing braided fibre bundles of electric lines of force through space and time. Thus there will be a unique set of such fibre bundles emerging from the molecule which, because of the way the electrons move within this structure, will also be vibrating in a pattern that is characteristic of the chemical. These bundles, as they move through space-time, will impose a pattern on the world-line web, which can then be communicated to the water molecules in which the chemical is dissolved. In each subsequent dilution process undertaken in producing a homoeopathic medicine there will be a branch point in space-time, but there will be clear channels which lead back to the original chemical even after there are no more molecules left in the final medicine. Thus the vibrational structure of the molecule, in space and time, will still be present in the end product. It is very likely that, after some length of time, the exposure of the medicine to naturally occurring electromagnetic radiation will erase this memory, but it is possible that it can be retained for a sufficient length of time to effect a cure.

Other Ideas on Cosmic or Universal Memories

The concept of a universal or cosmic memory is not new. It has taken a variety of different forms, at different times, and in different cultures. In this section we look, very briefly, at some of these ideas. In particular, we consider the similarities, and the differences, between the world-line-web memory and some other concepts.

1. The Akashic Record

The akashic record is the enduring trace of all events that have ever occurred. Every thought, every idea and every emotion is said to be preserved in the astral light. The word 'akashic' is from *akasha* in Sanskrit. In Hinduism it is used to denote the all-pervading and universal medium. Some Western writers have compared it to the 'ether', which in nineteenth-century physics was supposed to be an all-pervading medium carrying electromagnetic waves, just as the air transmits sound waves. The akashic record is rather more than the ether, in that it not only has a physical side to it, but it is also the record of all emotional and spiritual experiences. In this sense there is a closer link between the akashic record and the world-line web, in that it too records emotional experiences, although it in no way addresses itself to spiritual concepts and ideas. If such concepts ever do find a comfortable place in Western thought, they are very likely to lie outside the bounds of conventional orthodox science. On the other hand the world-line-web-memory concept is an attempt to bring certain paranormal concepts into the realm of conventional orthodox science. The basic ideas are still speculative, but all scientific theories start as speculative generalizations of experimental and observational data. Speculation is a necessary and important aspect of science, and it represents the positive side of scientific progress whereas scepticism, which is also necessary for progress, is the more negative side. Speculation and scepticism are the yin and yang of scientific development – and there is no true scientific understanding unless both sides are understood and accepted.

2. The Collective Unconscious

It was Carl Gustav Jung who introduced this term into psychology. It would be unfair to Jung's concept of the 'collective unconscious' to reduce it to the world-line-web concept of memory. However, there are some similarities between the two, although there are probably more differences. Jung used the term to designate a stratum of psychic activity which was below the level of the personal unconscious. The personal unconscious was seen as resting on the collective unconscious. The past experiences common to all and the acquired wisdom of the human species are all stored in the collective unconscious. Sometimes these experiences are projected from the collective unconscious, in dreams or in works of art. Symbolism is the language of the collective unconscious, especially the symbolism of 'archetypes'. The more a person submits to individuation – the more a person becomes himself or herself – the more he or she will vary from the collective norms, standards, precepts and values.

In the theory of the world-line web of memory we are all woven of the same superluminal fabric, but we are a unique and individual pattern within this fabric. The collections of genes which we inherited, the textures of our skins, the shapes of our bodies, our habits, our tastes and all our complex behaviour patterns, are what make us individuals, but we are connected to other members of our family, to members of our race, to other members of the human species, to our terrestrial environment and to the cosmos. We are thus ourselves, but also a part of the whole.

3. The Cosmic Reservoir of Memories

This was a term mentioned by the American psychologist, William James. At one stage of his career he investigated the well-known medium, Mrs Leonora Piper. His investigations convinced him that she was 'in possession of a power as yet unexplained'. James was an extremely influential psychologist in his day. He also played an important part in research into parapsychology, helping to found the American Society for Psychical Research. His investigation of Mrs Piper led him to suggest that she had a 'will to personate', to imitate or create a personality. He went on to propose that this will might be able to tap the memories of the sitters and perhaps even people not present at the session and 'possibly some cosmic reservoir in which the memories of earth are stored, whether in the shape of "spirits" or not'. I have not been able to find a more detailed development of James's concept of a cosmic reservoir of memory, but in this brief statement there do seem to be some similarities with the world-line web of memory.

Interconnection between Everything in the Universe

The interconnection between all things has, for hundreds of years, been very much a part of Eastern mysticism. Modern physics, in the form of the theory of relativity and quantum theory, has made the scientific discovery of this concept in the last few decades of our own century. It is then not surprising that there should exist parallels between Eastern mysticism and the current foundations of physics. These have been investigated by Fritjof Capra in his book *The Tao of Physics*, in which he says:

In the Eastern view then, as in the view of modern physics, everything in the universe is connected to everything else and no part of it is fundamental. The properties of any part are determined, not by some fundamental law, but by the properties of all the other parts. Both physicists and mystics realize the resulting impossibility of fully explaining any phenomena, but then they take different attitudes. Physicists, as discussed before, are satisfied with an approximate understanding of nature. The Eastern mystics, on the other hand, are not interested in approximate, or 'relative' knowledge. They are concerned with 'absolute' knowledge involving an understanding of the totality of Life.

Gary Zukav, in *The Dancing Wu Li Masters*, also draws attention to the similarities between modern physics and Eastern mysticism:

'Eastern religions' differ considerably among themselves. It would be a mistake to equate Hinduism, for example, with Buddhism, even though they are more like each other than either of them is like a religion of the West. None the less, all Eastern religions (psychologies) are compatible in a very fundamental way with Bohm's physics and philosophy. All of them are based upon the experience of a pure undifferentiated reality which is that-which-is.

Epilogue

The theory described and developed in this book is the result of an attempt to reconcile, at least within my own mind, the fundamental conflict between the theories of relativity and quantum theory. Like all theories, it is speculative, but it is underpinned by a mathematical framework, and so, with further developments and calculations, it will lead to results that can be tested against observations and experiments. However, even in its present state, it is able to offer explanations for a wide variety of physical phenomena. It also shows that it is possible to bring some phenomena, which up to now have been dismissed as paranormal, into the realm of scientific explanation. For me the most pleasing aspect of the theory is that it is a theory of reconciliation. Not only offering a way of reconciling relativity with quantum theory, but also the past with the present, the orthodox with the paranormal and the East with the West. If the presentation of the theory does nothing other than stimulate debate on these important questions, then the task which I set myself will have been fulfilled.

Much of what I believe about the scientific process, is contained in a few passages from a public address given by Richard Feynman to the National Academy of Sciences in 1955 and entitled *The Value of Science*. Feynman is the most successful theoretical physicist of the later half of the twentieth century. He can be rightly so called because his theories have been validated by observation and experiment. Some other physicists have been seen as the successors to Newton and Einstein, but even if their theories are couched in mathematically more sophisticated terms than those of Feynman, they remain unconfirmed by experimental and observational data, and so they cannot as yet be called successful theories. Feynman had this to say:

Our responsibility is to do what we can, learn what we can, improve the solutions, and pass them on. It is our responsibility to leave the people of the future a free hand ... It is our responsibility as scientists, knowing the great progress which comes from a satisfactory philosophy of ignorance, the great progress which is the fruit of freedom of thought, to proclaim the value of this freedom, to teach how doubt is not to be feared but welcomed and discussed; and to demand this freedom as our duty to all coming generations.

Feynman finds a secure place with the great thinkers of any age, not only because of his scientific achievements, which are great, but because of his humility and because he realizes that human understanding has its own limitations.

Bibliography

Introduction

Bohm, D., *Wholeness and the Implicate Order*, Routledge & Kegan Paul, 1980

Bronowski, J., *The Ascent of Man*, BBC, 1973

Davies, P. W. C., *Superstrings: A Theory for Everything*, Cambridge University Press, 1988

Dawkins, R., *The Blind Watchmaker*, Longman, 1986

Hallam, A., *Great Geological Controversies*, Oxford University Press, 1986

Herbert, N., *Quantum Reality*, Rider, 1985

Kuhn, T. S., *The Copernican Revolution*, Chicago University Press, 1962

Kuhn, T. S., *The Structure of Scientific Revolution*, Chicago University Press, 1970

Peacocke, A., *God and the New Biology*, Dent, 1986

Sheldrake, R., *The Presence of the Past*, Collins, 1988

Smith, C., and Best, S., *Electromagnetic Man*, Dent, 1989

Zukav, G., *The Dancing Wu Li Masters*, Rider Hutchinson, 1979

Chapter 1

Baker, R., *Human Navigation and the Sixth Sense*, Manchester University Press, 1981

Downer, J., *Supersense*, BBC, 1988

Chapter 2

Gregory, R., *Mind in Science*, Weidenfeld & Nicholson, 1981

Seymour, P. A. H., *Cosmic Magnetism*, Adam Hilger, 1986

Chapter 3

Cloudsley-Thompson, J. L., *Biological Clocks*, Weidenfeld & Nicholson, 1980

Ward, R. R., *The Living Clocks*, Collins, 1972

Chapter 4

Bell, J. S., *Speakable and Unspeakable in Quantum Mechanics*, Cambridge University Press, 1987
Bronowski, J., *The Ascent of Man*, BBC, 1973
Davies, P. W. C., *The Cosmic Blueprint*, Unwin, 1989
Hughes, R., *The Shock of the New*, BBC, 1980
Zukav, G., *The Dancing Wu Li Masters*, Rider Hutchinson, 1979

Chapter 5

Capra, F., *The Tao of Physics*, Fontana, 1983
Davies, P. C. W., *Superstrings: A Theory of Everything*, Cambridge University Press, 1988

Chapter 6

Seymour, P. A. H., *Cosmic Magnetism*, Adam Hilger, 1986

Chapter 7

Seymour, P. A. H., *Cosmic Magnetism*, Adam Hilger, 1986
Seymour, P. A. H., *Astrology: The Evidence of Science*, Arkana, 1990

Chapter 8

Sheldrake, R., *A New Science of Life*, Blond & Briggs, 1981
Sheldrake, R., *The Presence of the Past*, Collins, 1988
Zukav, G., *The Dancing Wu Li Masters*, Rider Hutchinson, 1979

Chapter 9

Brookesmith, P., ed., *When the Impossible Happens*, Orbis Publishing, 1984
Cavendish, R., ed., *Encyclopedia of the Unexplained*, Arkana, 1989

Chapter 10

Holroyd, S., ed., *The Arkana Dictionary of New Perspectives*, Arkana, 1989

Inglis, B., *The Paranormal*, Paladin, 1986

Smith, C., and Best, S., *Electromagnetic Man*, Dent, 1989

Chapter 11

Roberts, P., *The Message of Astrology*, Aquarian Press, 1990

Roy, A. E., *A Sense of Something Strange*, Dog & Bone, 1991

Seymour, P. A. H., *Astrology: The Evidence of Science*, Arkana, 1990

Thornton, P., *The Forces of Destiny*, Weidenfeld & Nicholson, 1990

Zukav, G., *The Dancing Wu Li Masters*, Rider Hutchinson, 1979

Chapter 12

Capra, F., *The Tao of Physics*, Fontana, 1983

Smith, C., and Best, S., *Electromagnetic Man*, Dent, 1989

Epilogue

Feynman, R. P., *What Do You Care What Other People Think?*, Unwin Hyman, 1988

Index